the**overcast's**

GUIDE TO
BEERS
of
NEWFOUNDLAND

The Definitive Guide
to **Beer on The Rock**

BREAKWATER

Contents

WHAT'S IN A BEER?

Beer is 4 Ingredients Rung Through 4 Processes

BEER IS GENERALLY MADE BY USING 4 INGREDIENTS THAT ARE rung through 4 different processes. Those 4 ingredients are water, hops, yeast, and a starch grain that is usually barley.

By "usually barley," we mean that the starch grain used to make beer is normally barley. But sometimes, as in a wheat ale like Storm's Rapsberry Wheat Ale, it's wheat instead of barley. YellowBelly once made a "Rye PA" instead of an IPA by substituting Rye for Barley, and Bootleg Brewing use rye in their El Diablo Rojo instead of barley. Sometimes it's a combination of grains: Port Rexton's Gardener Gose ale, for example, uses a combination of wheat and barley. Mixing up the type and amount of barley used, or substituting barley altogether with something like rye or wheat or rice, is a way to vary the flavour of a beer.

ST. JOHN'S BEER TOURS Kayla Walters of St. John's Beer Tours offers a variety of ways to taste local beers.

The Brewing Process

1. MAKING MALT FROM YOUR GRAIN The first step in making beer is to extract the sugars from your barley (or grain of choice). This process is called malting, and it produces The Malt. Basically, the barley is soaked in a large vat, heated, and then dried. Malting draws out the classic malty flavours of a beer (biscuits, caramel, chocolate, honey, etc), which are later balanced by the bitterness of adding hops to the mix. The more you dry out your barley in this phase, the darker and more toasted the ensuing beer will look and taste.

2. MAKING WORT FROM YOUR MALT The next step is called mashing. Basically, you steep your malt in hot water to make it release all of its sugars. At the end of this steeping process, you strain it, throw out the spent grains, and what remains is a sweet and sticky concoction called The Wort, which is pre-hopped (too sweet), pre-fermented (non-alcoholic) beer.

3. HOPPING THE WORT The wort is boiled for an hour or so, and during this phase a brewer will counter the sweetness of their wort with hops. Hops are green buds of plant material. They add varying degrees of bitterness to a beer, in order to balance its sweetness. There are many varieties of hops, so, how much hops are added, what variety or varieties of hops are added, and how often during this process they're added, greatly affect the beer's flavour. Conveniently, hops act as natural preservatives as well.

4. FERMENTING HOPPED WORT WITH YEAST Once the hopped wort has cooled, it is strained and filtered and transferred to a fermenting tank. At this point a brewer selects a strain of yeast, adds it to the wort, and as the yeast have a feast on it, they produce alcohol and CO_2 in a process known as fermentation. Yeast are living beings, so a brewer must keep them happy and cater to things like the ideal fermenting temperature for the strain of yeast being used. The type of yeast used, and the fermentation temperature, will affect the flavour of the beer.

If All Beer Is Made This Way, Why Do They All Taste Different?

PLENTY OF REASONS. For starters, the endless types of grain, hops, water, and yeast a brewer can use, and the countless combinations to use them in. Also, the temperatures and durations used in each brewing process will affect taste. Plus, you're allowed to add over 100 other ingredients to your beer in Canada (in addition to grain, yeast, hops, and water). These are typically referred to as adjuncts, and include the corn or rice many large breweries use as filler to save on costs. But they also include adventurous additions, like the turnip YellowBelly once used in their temporarily available Turnip Pale Ale. Variety is the spice of life *and* beer.

Lagers Versus Ales:

The Two Categories of Beer

THERE ARE COUNTLESS *STYLES* OF BEER, BUT EVERY BEER IS EITHER A LAGER OR AN ALE.

It's easy to compare the duality of lagers and ales to white wines and red wines. There are many kinds of wine, but ultimately, there is red and there is white. Like white wines, lagers are crisp, clean, smooth, and easy drinking. And like red wines, ales have more flavours, complexity, and fuller bodies.

COMMON STYLES OF LAGERS Lagers, Pilsners, Dunkels, Bocks, Oktoberfest beers

COMMON STYLES OF ALES Ales, IPAs, Stouts, Porters, Red Ales, Brown Ales, Wheat Beers (Witbier), Blonde Ales, Sour Ales, Cream Ales, Saisons, Kolsch

Major Difference No. 1
THE STRAIN OF YEAST USED TO BREW THEM

There are hundreds of types of yeast, just like there are many breeds of dog. Using artificial selection, humans have specialized different strains of yeast for brewing beer. Some to make ales with, some to make lagers with.

The strain of yeast used in brewing a beer will greatly affect its flavour. This is especially true for ales, because lager yeasts impart less flavour on their beer. Yeasts used to make ales are called "top-fermenting yeasts" and yeasts used to make lagers are called "bottom-fermenting yeasts." It's as straight-forward as it sounds; during fermentation, ale yeasts tend to rise to the surface during fermentation, lager yeasts tend to sink to the bottom. As an example of how this affects the final product, ales end

up having a thicker, richer head than lagers.

This is a simplified explanation, and brewers complicate this by, say, using a bottom-fermenting yeast to make an atypical ale.

Major Difference No. 2
FERMENTING TEMPERATURE AND DURATION

Brewers ferment ale yeasts at a higher temperature than a lager yeast, because ale yeasts, like Floridians, prefer higher temperatures. Not hot, just higher, roughly room temperature. This means ales ferment and mature faster than lagers.

Lagers are fermented at lower temps,for longer periods of time. The very term "lagering" means "to store," since lagers

were traditionally left to ferment for so long. The combination of colder temperatures and bottom-fermenting yeasts are why a lager has a relatively milder taste than an ale, and why they are more crisp and easy drinking than an ale.

Because they're fermented at higher temperatures, ales end up higher in chemicals called esters, and those esters are a distinctive character of ales. As an example, acetaldehyde imparts a green-apple aroma. Some ale yeasts give off a presence of clove, where others mark a beer with things as unique as banana (as in German Hefeweizens).

Some brewers, for some of their beers, will opt to employ a process of "Cold Lagering" on their ales, to smooth over their flavours. This is pretty standard for Cream Ales, like Quidi Vidi's Eric's Cream Ale, and Western Newfoundland Brewing's Wild Cove Cream Ale.

A HISTORY
OF BEER IN
NEWFOUNDLAND

1800-1962:

The Major Players of the Past Still Linger on Today

BACK IN THE 1800S, RIGHT UP UNTIL THE 1960S, THE BREWERY scene of Newfoundland was composed solely of small, local, and independent breweries making beer for the people of the province.

A variety of homegrown brewers came and went during the 1800s and 1900s, but three lasted the longest and made the biggest mark on the history of brewing in Newfoundland, and as you'll read, their influence still marks our province's beer preferences tothis day. These breweries were Bavarian Brewing, Bennett Brewing, and Newfoundland Brewery.

None of them are around anymore, because all three of them were bought out when a cross-Canada wave of big national brewers buying out local ones came crashing down on Newfoundland. In the same year, 1962, Molson, Labatt, and Carling-O'Keefe bought one Newfoundland brewery apiece.

Despite their demise, the presence of Bennett Brewing, Newfoundland Brewery, and Bavarian Brewing lives on today, literally, as some of the beers they created are still brewed here, and only here, by Molson and Labatt.

WELCOME TO
NFLD'S YOUNGEST CITY
FROM
NFLD'S OLDEST BREWERY

THE BENNETT BREWING
CO. LTD.

BREWERS OF

THE **3** BIG

DOMINION ALE
DOMINION STOUT
RAINBOW BEER

A. R. BURRY LTD.   DISTRIBUTOR

AT YOUR SERVICE
DIAL 22005

(NOT INSERTED BY THE BLC)

JANUARY, 1956   23

WELCOME TO CORNER BROOK A 1956 ad in the *Atlantic Guardian* of Bennett welcoming Newfoundland's newest city.

Labatt continues to brew Blue Star and Jockey Club (creations of Bavarian Brewing) and Molson still brews India and Dominion Ale (creations of Newfoundland Brewery and Bennett Brewing respectively) as well as Black Horse, which Bennett Brewing made, though did not create.

These Newfoundland-born beers were so beloved by locals, that brewers like Molson and Labatt knew better than to cancel them. Newfoundlanders might be friendly, but it's equally true we don't like change 'round here. Besides, it's bad business to discontinue well-branded, top-selling beers.

There were, of course, other local breweries who came and went in Newfoundland's history, like Lindberg Brewing Company and Kavanaugh and Company. The later made their own beer, but were perhaps most beloved for importing Guinness into Newfoundland. But these breweries were blips to the game-changers that were Bavarian Brewing, Bennett Brewing, and Newfoundland Brewery.

BAVARIAN BREWING

The Trendsetters Who Gave Us Blue Star and Jockey Club

1932—1962

Bavarian Brewing (1932-1962) can be thanked for creating Blue Star and Jockey Club, which still exist to this day in Newfoundland and Newfoundland only.

They may also take credit for creating the average Newfoundlander's preference for light lagers that go down easy. Our province is the nation's biggest consumer of light lagers, and history can trace that back to one German Brewmaster's influence on local beer in the 1900s.

When Bavarian Brewing opened for business in 1932, Newfoundland was still getting back into the swing of brewing beers again, after years of prohibition. There were only two post-prohibition players left on the beer scene here, Bennett Brewing and Newfoundland Brewery. Both of them were exclusively making ales, so the island's beer scene was dominated by their English-style pale ales and stouts, which makes sense for an English-settled colony.

Little did these two breweries know, there was a real demand in North America for easier-drinking beers at this time. No one in Newfoundland was making much in the way of lagers. Signal-Hill-based Lindberg Brewery had been onto this trend ahead of the curve, making light "Bavarian style" lagers, but the company died right before prohibition, or because of prohibition, depending on your source.

Needless to say, there was room for revolution in the local brewing scene, and Bavarian Brewing seized that opportunity. Bavarian found their niche in offering locals crisp and refreshing lagers, like the kinds that sell so well in Newfoundland today: Blue Star, Quidi Vidi Iceberg, Coors Light, etc.

Garrett Brownrigg, a man described by his son as someone who was "always going for something," decided to expand his soft-drink business into a brewery, and brew, specifically, German "Bavarian-style" beers. Reportedly on a whim, Brownrigg went to Germany seeking the right German brewmaster for the job of introducing authentic German-style lagers to the people of Newfoundland. He came back with a man named Brehm, Brehm's wife, and blueprints for a true German lager brewery.

To their own demise, Brownrigg and Brehm were dead set on decking out the brewery in German-imported machinery, a costly endeavour at that time, which is why Brownrigg went broke constructing the plant, and Brehm spooked off into obscurity after 75% of the plant was constructed.

A merchant named Albert E. Hickman liked the vision though, and he came to own Brownrigg Brewery, which he renamed Bavarian Brewing. If the name Albert E. Hickman rings a bell, it's because he's the same man who launched Hickman Motors. Albert brought one of the first cars to Newfoundland; he bought it in New York, shipped it home on a schooner, and others started wanting them, so he started selling them. He was also prime minister for a month in 1924.

Hickman found himself a German brewmaster named Hans Schneider. Schneider was a meticulous man who truly put the master in brewmaster. Back then, you had to be a master of your craft, as brewers did not have the quality-control technology available today.

Schneider went on to win awards for his creations like Jockey Club and Black Munich, both created in his small apartment above the brewery. He made Bavarian Brewing Newfoundland's wealthiest, most popular brewery.

Bavarian Brewery's success with lagers was so well received that Newfoundland's other brewers couldn't ignore it, and scrambled to recruit some Germans of their own, to come and overhaul their beer lists. This created a frenzy among Newfoundland's big three brewers—Bavarian, Newfoundland Brewery, and Bennett—to create the ultimate German-style beers.

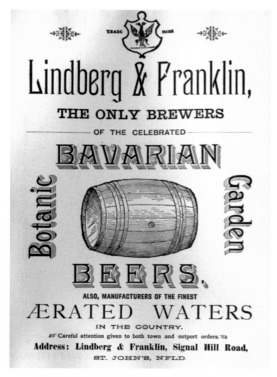

A LOCAL CASUALTY OF PROHIBITION

As this ad shows, Lindberg & Franklin were ahead of Bavarian Brewing in their efforts to introduce "Bavarian style lagers" to Newfoundland. But prohibition prohibited their efforts.

THE EVOLUTION OF BLUE STAR: 1960S TO 2012

These bottles capture a change in ownership and logos for the storied Blue Star brand over the years.

The German brewmasters at the helms of all three major Newfoundland brewers during these decades became our island's taste-makers, and if you love your Blue Star or Coors or QV Light, you can thank the German influence on the history of local brewing. Blue Star was actually a creation of Bavarian Brewing, and won the Munich Gold Medal in Germany in 1954, so even the Germans loved Newfoundland's German-influenced Newfoundland beer.

Bavarian Brewery was located on Leslie Street in St. John's, where the Labatt brewery currently operates, and that's not a coincidence: Labatt bought these guys out in 1962, but kept on making Blue Star and Jockey Club because Newfoundlanders loved them so much. Whether it's a coincidence or not, there's a small street near the brewery called Brownrigg Place, likely after the man who was the impetus of Bavarian Brewing.

In addition to Jockey Club and Blue Star, Bavarian brewed popular beers like Dark Munich, Irish Style Porter, Red Label, and Black Label, but Blue Star was always their pride, joy, and name-maker.

BENNETT BREWING
Newfoundland's Longest Lived Brewery

1827—1962

Bennett Brewing created Dominion Ale, and in a very roundabout way, were responsible for Black Horse becoming a Newfoundland-only beer, despite Black Horse being created in Quebec. That's a long story: see the page on Black Horse beer for that one.

Bennett Brewing Company was founded way back in 1827 by a colourful character named Charles Fox Bennett, though it was called Riverhead Brewery back in its founding days. Charles came here by way of England, and did a lot more for the province than brew it some great beer. He went on to become premier of Newfoundland, and yes, if you're reading this book in order and paying attention, that means two brewery founders in NL history went on to be leaders of our province.

Moreover, Charles Fox Bennett went down in the history books as the man who established mining as an economic engine for our economy, and he also fought like hell to successfully keep Newfoundland out of Canada during his leadership of the anti-Confederate Party in 1869's election.

Charles died in the early 1880s, and oddly enough, through sheer coincidence, the man who took over Bennett Brewing was of no relation, but did share the last name of Bennett. Edward W. Bennett took it over in 1884. During Bennett Brewing's 135 years of independent operation, its biggest challenge came 90 years after it was founded, and that challenge was weathering the storm of prohibition.

In Newfoundland, prohibition lasted from 1917-1924. Bennett survived by going dormant for over a year, and when it reopened in 1918, it was selling near beers of 2% or less alcohol, until 1924, as this was deemed legal during prohibition.

DOMINION PALE ALE C. 1970S As this label indicates, Dominion was a pale ale when Bennett Brewing were making it. Today, under Molson's ownership, it's a lager. Your grandparent's Dominion was nothing like yours.

Right after prohibition ended, the company started making strong and proper beers again, and among them, Dominion Ale emerged as a favourite. Had they not weathered that storm, Dominion Ale never would've been a thing in every cooler in every corner store in Newfoundland, as it is to this day.

In its post-Prohibition heyday, Bennett Brewing was best known for what they marketed as Newfoundland's "Big 3 Beers": Dominion Pale Ale, Dominion Stout, and Rainbow Beer. They were also very well known for Haig Ale. Rainbow Beer was marketed with a locally coloured pun, "A rainbow at night, a sailor's Delight."

Canadian mega-brewery Carling O'Keefe bought Bennett Brewing in 1962, but, because they were a Toronto-based company, they used Bennett's Brewery as their plant of operation in St. John's, and continued to brew some of Bennett's beers, like Dominion Ale, alongside its own brands that it introduced to Newfoundland, like Extra Old Stock (which was available here into the 2000s).

In 1989, to get a leg up on Labatt, Molson merged with Carling-O'Keefe, as Molson and Carling-O'Keefe were the 2nd and 3rd largest brewers in the country at the time. The Bennett brewery was closed at this time, and now the only remnant of Bennett's century-and-a-half-long stint as our longest-standing brewery, is Dominion Ale. May it, for this reason, never go extinct. Molson continues to make the stuff to this day in its St. John's plant, and its bottles still feature the Bennett logo and name on their labels as a heritage homage.

In addition to their beer, Bennett Brewing produced a well-known and much-loved Newfoundland Songbook series. There were 10 volumes published during the 1950s, 60s, and 70s. This was largely a super smart marketing move. For decades, during the late 1900s, various local beer brands fought each other to be seen as the most legit true brew of Newfoundland, and these song books were a way for Bennett to thread itself into our culture's strong ties to music.

The songbooks promoted, celebrated, shared, and kept alive the music of Newfoundland. These songbooks were stuck into boxes of Dominion Ale with the beer as a freebie. You can still find these old songbooks in some outport towns, deep in their libraries, your nan's piano bench, or sacredly preserved in a desk drawer.

THE NEWFOUNDLAND SONGBOOK SERIES
While Bennett Brewing's songbooks helped preserve and disseminate the music of Newfoundland, it was also a brilliant marketing strategy that associated the brewery with a sense of cultural pride.

NEWFOUNDLAND BREWERY

Creators of Your Favourite Local Macrobrew, India Beer

1893–1962

Only one of Newfoundland Brewery Limited's beers is still brewed today, but it's the one consistently voted by readers of *The Overcast* as the "Best Local Macrobrew": India Beer. Their brewery was located on Elizabeth Avenue. Molson bought them out in 1962, and India Beer is all that remains of Newfoundland Brewery's stint from 1893-1962.

The other heavy hitters these guys made were Irish Cream Porter, and India Pale Ale, which was a totally different beer than India Beer, so yes, that's right, India Beer is NOT an IPA. India Beer is actually a lager; a lighter version of the now extinct India Pale Ale, which also had a Newfoundland dog on its label for a while. Some other brands this company made were a Moose Ale and a Red Top Golden Amber Ale.

Prior to the 1930s, Newfoundland Brewery Limited, and its only real competitor, Bennett Brewing, had it knocked as the two kingpin brewers in town. They were making similar kinds of beer: English-style ales. But in the early 1930s, when Bavarian Brewing erupted onto the local scene, brewing German-style, easy drinking lagers, Bavarian's instant success spurred Newfoundland Brewery to mimic Bavarian's output of German-style lagers.

Newfoundland Brewery quickly recruited a German Brewmaster, and brought in all new equipment from The States to reboot and rebrand themselves. Brewmaster Otto Scheffhauser was a 6 foot 6 beast of a brewmaster, clocking in at 240 pounds, who took his craft as seriously as your nan takes her tea biscuits.

Otto took total control of the operation, and really put it into high gear, so to speak (if you caught the Otto/Auto pun). There are verifiable accounts of the brewery's owners being scared to step foot in the building if Otto was there, for fear of disturbing him, as Otto didn't like to be interrupted from his diligent devotion to his craft.

INDIA BEER BOTTLE c. 1970s. Contrary to popular folklore, India Beer is not named after the dog on its label. The proof is in the history of labels: India existed long before its logo was a Newfoundland Dog. Maybe the dog was named after the beer? [Photo: India Beer - The Obsolescence Project by Deanne Achong - projectobso.com]

You can't blame him given the times: the brewing technology that exists today was not even conceivable back then. To test the success of yeast converting starch to sugar, for instance, he'd pour a little on a seat and sit on it to make sure it was "tacky enough." A far cry from how things are done today. It was from this serious-as-a-stroke attention to detail and devotion to craft that your beloved India Beer was brewed.

PORT REXTON	F-F
QUIDI VIDI	S DO
SPLIT ROCK	F SMC
STORM	IRIS
YELLOW BELLY	F

TODAY'S LOCAL BREWERIES

The Post-62 Resurgence of Microbreweries

THE AFOREMENTIONED 1962 BUY-OUT OF ALL LOCAL BREWERS
by big-league national brewers was the end of independent, local breweries in Newfoundland & Labrador. It was a Canada-wide trend of local breweries going the way of the dodo.

Even though brewers like Molson and Labatt have kept some of our old breweries' beers on by name—India, Blue Star, Jockey Club, Dominion, and Black Horse—some recipe and methodology changes were inevitably made by these brewers, to align them with their own brands, markets, and brewing methods. In fact, some of these beers have changed so radically they're lagers now, where once they were ales. As one former employee of Bennett Brewing attested during research for this book, "Dominion Ale has been a lager since at least the mid-seventies."

Until you find an old bottle in Nan's basement somewhere, you'll never know what an India, Jockey Club, Black Horse, Blue Star, or Dominion of yesteryear really tasted like, relative to their new iteration. Still, plenty of us love these nostalgic brews as they are today: we grew up on them, and they ain't bad. Most anyone reading this book has a favourite between India, Jockey Club, Black Horse, Blue Star, or Dominion Ale.

But back in the 90s, two local breweries, Storm Brewing and Quidi Vidi Brewery, started introducing some new local beers into the mix, starting the craft beer boom here that has slowly but surely exploded in recent years. Between 2016-2017 the number of local microbreweries in Newfoundland tripled; 13 more are set to open in 2018 or 2019.

We're catching up to the craft boom of Canada. According to the *Financial Post*, between 2006 and 2014, the number of Canadian microbreweries grew sixfold to 520, infusing the market with a vast diversity of new, quality beers. Market shares between the big international macrobreweries and small local microbreweries are slowly leveling out.

Here on the rock, as of the publication date of this book, there are more breweries in Newfoundland than ever: 9 microbreweries, and 3 national macrobreweries. The boom is booming, and 12 more breweries will open their doors within a year of this book's publication: most imminently, Dildo Brewing in Dildo, Firehall Brewery in St. John's, Secret Cove on the Port-au Port Peninsula, and Motion Bay Brewing in Petty Harbour.

Ironically, it was a monopoly of megabrewers turning Canada's beer output into a sea of sameness that played a huge role in the recent craft beer revolution. While there's nothing wrong with pledging allegiance to your Molson Canadian or Alexander Keith's, variety is the spice of life, and the variety of beers in Canada was seriously lacking by the 1990s. There was no one making West Coast IPAs, Coffee Porters, Goses, Ciders... leaving niches unfilled.

During the decades-long lull in local craft brewing, world-travelling beer enthusiasts would encounter interesting ales and come back with tales to tell from beer beyond our borders. Enough of these people wanted to make and sell those kinds of beers, to cash in on wide open niches.

Also, 1989's free-trade agreement between Canada and the US worked in microbreweries' favour. The free trade agreement allowed imported US beers to be sold in Canada, exposing us to more options, and giving big Canadian brewers some dangerous new competition.

Microbreweries responded to this macrobrewery struggle (of increased competition between big league brewers) by marketing the strengths of craft beers. At a time when big brewers were struggling to offer the cheapest or most popular beer, the little brewers were appealing to quality over cost of beer, and promoting themselves to beer

lovers, instead of deal lovers. It was a smart, viable way to compete for sales and interest.

Decades of limited beer options put demand for something different back on the table, and enough people filled that demand. Now it's impossible to keep up with the temporarily available Canadian craft beer offerings the NLC, or the gossip of new micro-breweries set to open here.

Demand for variety and new things bred opportunity, and microbreweries started popping up again, including here in Newfoundland. Today, Quidi Vidi successfully runs with the giants Molson and Labatt, as our third biggest producer of beer, and they're on tap or in stores just about everywhere on the island. Port Rexton are so run off their heads with orders, they had to buy two new double-sized fermenters before their first anniversary.

Today, there are well over 600 Canadian microbreweries, with more opening their doors every month, and that's a far cry from where we were in the early 1980s, when there were only ten Canadian brewers controlling the beer game in the country. The three largest, Molson, Labatt and Carling O'Keefe owned a whopping 96% of the market.

Today the market is increasingly more fairly shared, and there's something to whet all of our palates. But as of 2016, Molson Coors owns about 35% of the Canadian market, and Anheuser-Busch InBev (who owns Labatt) owns 42%. That means the other 600+ Canadian breweries only get 33% of sales. So drink local and broadly to keep all these new breweries coming.

THE RISE OF CRAFT BEER IN CANADA Today, there are well over 600 Canadian microbreweries. The Atlantic provinces produce many of the country's best beers, like Good Robot, Garrison, and Picaroon's. Beau's, Driftwood, and Muskoka are three pioneering mainland craft breweries worth a shout out here.

ATLANTIC BREWERY / BISON BREWING

1968–1973

There was one short-lived pre-1990s stab at getting a local craft-beer operation off the ground: Atlantic Brewery.

After the American Air Force withdrew its operations in Stephenville, the town needed to start plotting ways of revitalizing itself. The idea of a brewery emerged, to create some jobs and make use of old, empty buildings. 2.5 million dollars was spent to set up a cutting-edge brewery, and it employed about 50 locals, who worked together to create a competitive, impressive, modern operation. They were best known for Atlantic Lager and Atlantic Draft.

But problems came as soon as one year later, and forced a disastrous lull in production. Staff had to be culled for financial reasons. Hearing tell of their financial woes, Bison Petroleum and Minerals LTD. made an offer to buy them out in 1970.

The newly named Bison Brewing managed to double production, and then invested $150,000 more into their operation, in order to start exporting their beer into the northeast section of the United States, as that demographic was known to be an avid consumer of Canadian beer.

But in Newfoundland, if it's not a fire, it's a flood that kills a good thing in the food and drink business. In 1973, a flood in the facility did so much damage to their brewery it was deemed unviable to keep the operation going. It would've cost about a million bucks to get it back on track, and Bison Petroleum were hauling out of Stephenville anyway, so that was that for Bison Brewery.

However, the establishment of this brewery is credited with revitalizing the town's economy, and allowed Labatt to set up shop in the brewery in 1974 until 1981, which employed locals. These same workers were transferred to St. John's when Labatt congregated in the capital city. There are still bottles kicking around in antique shops that show local Labatt-brewed beers as being "brewed in Stephenville."

LAGER AND ALE Bison Brewery produced two primary beers. Their flagship was Atlantic Lager. It came in a pretty simple stubby with the Atlantic Brewery's logo. Draft bottles are considerably more rare. Considering the short lifespan of the brewery, it's remarkable that any survived at all!

BOOTLEG BREW CO.

2017, CORNER BROOK

A couple of cooks from Corner Brook cooked up the idea of bringing the best tastes of Canadian craft beer to their hometown of Corner Brook.

Co-founders Matt Tilley and Morgan Turner met while working in the food industry at Corner Brook's famed Newfound Sushi. They each moved away, continuing to cook in various restaurants, where they were exposed to a world of beer beyond the Black Horse they grew up on.

Being exposed to some of the country's best craft beers got them excited about a switch from food to the brewing biz. For Matt, it was breweries like Oast House, Beaus, Collective Arts, and Le Trou de Diable that got him hooked on homebrewing. For Morgan it was places like Picaroons, Phillips, Brewdog, Rouge, and Boxing Rock. They both converge on Flying Monkeys

After moving back home, they spent time developing recipes, foraging for local ingredients to complement some of them, and teaching themselves to brew the kind of beer they'd gotten used to drinking up in Canada.

During their time in the food industry, they say they noticed that "more and more, people like to know where their food and drink come from." With a local microbrew, you can trust there's nothing sketchy in your beer. Using skills they gained from years behind the line, they developed beers to complement food.

"We have about seventeen years between us working in the restaurant industry," they say, "so it's just a natural bridge for us." Speaking of food, while they plan on focussing on the beer for the first while, they will expand into offering food that works well with their beers. Their taproom offers taster flights, pints, and growlers, and you can find their beers in a few restaurants as well. In time, they may start bottling for the NLC.

After experimenting amply with recipes, they crafted 20 different brews, but whittled it

SAMPLES TO ST. JOHN'S Bootleg Brew Co.'s homebase taproom is located at 92 West Street in Corner Brook. But these custom sampler cases sent around to St. John's restaurants imply we can look forward to raising a glass of Bootleg elsewhere on the island. [Wood burning by Erin Tilley and Derek Tilley]

down to their top three to launch with. "These were our personal favourites, can be drank year round, and are different enough to hopefully give everybody something they will enjoy," Matt says.

"We will definitely be expanding into more styles when we work out the logistics with our space and equipment." They launched offering Hoppy Roger IPA, El Diablo Rojo (an amber rye ale), and East Coast Pale Ale.

They also offer seasonals or small batch runs meant to showcase the best that Newfoundland's natural bounty has to offer. "We've experimented a lot with whatever ingredients we could find, or were given to us by friends. Some of our personal favourites were our spruce tip session ale, partridgeberry saison, and blueberry ale."

They work with a local forager throughout the year to source goods for their

East Coast Pale Ale

ABV & TYPE: 5.1% American Pale Ale

APPEARANCE: Bright and hazy

AROMA: Floral and citrus

TEXTURE: Smooth for its style

TASTE: A clear grapefruit finish

BEHIND THE BEER: "We wanted to make a sessionable beer that was also very flavourful and well balanced," says the Bootleg duo, "something that could also be a good starter beer for those who may be new to craft beer here in Newfoundland."

East Coast Pale Ale is a smooth and easy drinking pale ale with a citrus-forward taste. Bootleg dry hop their pale ale with hops normally reserved for bittering. Doing so gives this beer its prominent tropical fruit aroma.

As for the beer label, they confess "we can't draw very well ourselves and figured it'd be a cool community effort thing to have friends design the logos for us." Local artist Erin Tilley designed this one.

seasonals, like Labrador tea and bakeapples. They bottle some of their seasonals and small batches in 750 ML bottles for sale at their taproom.

As for the name, Bootleg Brewing Co., "We wanted something that would reflect the history of our province, tying into the prohibition era, and something that would stick in people's minds."

El Diablo Rojo

ABV & TYPE: 5.8% Red Rye Ale

APPEARANCE: A deep, rich amber colour

AROMA: Sweet malts and a little spice

TEXTURE: Medium bodied

TASTE: A subtly spicy profile from the rye, that's balanced with deep caramel and chocolate flavours

BEHIND THE BEER: The El Diablo Rojo is "named after a joke nickname given to Matt by his manager, Ian Field, when he was running a food truck in Hamilton. We thought it suited the colour and slight spice flavour that was present in the beer."

The beer was a welcome addition to the beers of Newfoundland when the brewery opened, as there weren't many of its kind on the market when they launched theirs. For the design of their beer labels, Bootleg Brew Co. farmed it out to local artists. "Whenever we decide that a test batch is exactly what we wanted, we give samples to one of our artist friends and give them free reign to design artwork

that they feel fits the style and flavour of the beer." The El Diablo Rojo label was designed by local artist Sarah Whiffen.

Hoppy Roger IPA

ABV & TYPE: 6.2% IPA

APPEARANCE: Bronze and relatively opaque

AROMA: Complex fruit and floral aromas

TEXTURE: Medium bodied

TASTE: Carefully balanced with 4 types of grains and 3 hop varieties, yielding a slightly bitter beer with fruity, toffee, and pear notes

BEHIND THE BEER: Morgan is very much a fan of IPAs, but Matt not so much. Like all good partners-in-business, they compromised and crafted a recipe they both loved. The result is not your typical, raspy, notably bitter IPA. It's hoppy, yet easy drinking.

Local artist Jessie Donaldson was given a pint of Hoppy Roger and asked to create its label based on the beer's taste and style.

DILDO BREWING, TAP ROOM & MUSEUM

2018, DILDO

Brother and sister Angie and Roger George, and their spouses Rob and Debbie, set out to start a microbrewery in their hometown of Dildo, and wound up securing a unique homebase for it: The Dildo Museum.

The museum had a solid cultural heritage, but was in need of reinvigoration and repairs. After 20 years of running it, the museum's current owners, The Society of United Fishermen Lodge 84, could no longer maintain or operate it. So the George siblings and their spouses proposed to take over operations. Renovations reworked the space to be equal parts museum and brewhouse, with a taproom so visitors can sample local beer while sampling local history.

The museum is home to a lot of information on archaeological digs, and is heavy on artifacts pertaining to Maritime Archaic Indians (dating back to 3000 BC.), Dorset Eskimo, and Beothuk history, as well as interpretation of the 19th century cod fish hatchery that was located in Dildo, and more (including a lot of memorabilia that was contributed by residents of the town and the area over many years).

This 3-in-1 project of saving a museum, launching a brewery, and creating a real community hub for tourists and locals alike, made Dildo Brewing Company, Tap Room, and Museum a solid pick to win *The Overcast*'s $12,5000 Albedo Grant, which helped them completely redesign the museum within the brewery building.

With this book being published months before the brewery opened, we could not run their beer list yet, as they hadn't settled on one yet, they will launch with 4 core beers.

SOMETHING FOR EVERYONE "We all have different tastes, and we all enjoy different styles, depending on the season or occasion," Dildo Brewing's suite of beers will reflect their varied tastes, and no doubt offer something for everyone.

"We all have different tastes, and we all enjoy different styles, depending on the season or occasion," Angie says, so their suite of beers will reflect their varied tastes, and no doubt offer something for everyone when they open their doors in Spring 2018. We can say that during a photoshoot with Dildo Brewing, we were treated to a very nice porter and saison.

Like many new breweries popping up in Newfoundland (say, Port Rexton Brewing, or Scudrunner Brewery), Dildo Brewing Company was borne of a homebrewing hobby turned professional endeavour. "Roger had the idea," Angie says. His love of beer, then homebrewing, was largely inspired by visiting many breweries in Florida—Florida has well over 100 breweries, many of them amazing.

Dildo's two-storey space houses a taproom upstairs, in a big, open room with large windows looking out onto the ocean and Dildo Island; it's a quintessential Newfoundland view. Smokers or folks looking for some fresh air can roam around the building's wrap-around deck and long wharf, filling their phones with Instagrammable photos.

There's plans for a kitchen, and to have live entertainment regularly. So it's a true cultural hub in all senses: microbrewery, museum, and arts venue with a stunning view, bound to haul plenty of tourists and baycationers in off the highway.

"The vision for this museum, combined with our microbrewery operation is phenomenal to us. What excites us most is the impact we can have on the community of Dildo and the Avalon Peninsula." The feel of the museum atmosphere goes throughout the brewery and the taproom.

LABATT

1962, ST. JOHN'S

It ws 1962 when the country's biggest brewery, Labatt, set up shop in Newfoundland. They made their entrance into Newfoundland by buying out Newfoundland's famed Bavarian Brewing, and set up shop in their brewery on Leslie Street.

To this day, Labatt continues to brew Bavarian's two bestsellers, Blue Star and Jockey Club. They're brewed here and only here by Labatt, and remain serious local favourites. You can find them in every corner store or NLC on the island.

The history of Labatt's national operations date back to 1828 in London, Ontario, when John Balkwill opened London Brewery on Simcoe Street. It produced a mere 400 barrels of beer a year, most of which was sold through his tavern.

In 1847, Samuel Eccles purchased the operation from Balkwill, and partnered with his friend John Kinder Labatt, an Irish immigrant and well-studied brewmaster. Labatt turned the brewery into a hit, bumped up its production ten-fold, and bought out Eccles by 1853.

When John Labatt died in 1866, John Labatt II took over, and took the brewery to new heights in two ways. Firstly, by embracing the very latest in brewing technology (things like pasteurization and ice-making), and secondly, by using national and international competitions to raise brand awareness and relevancy.

In the mid 1870s, Labatt gained national buzz when its IPA took the silver medal at the Dominion of Canada Exposition in Ottawa. From there it started winning awards world-wide in the US, France, England, and Australia. This included an 1878 gold medal for Labatt India Pale Ale at the International Exposition in Paris.

By 1900, a third generation of Labatts had started spreading Labatt products further across the country, into the Maritimes, Manitoba, and the Northwest Territories. When prohibition levelled Ontario, and the country, from 1916-1927, dozens of Ontario breweries died off, but Labatt found a way to weather the dry spell.

Luckily for them, Ontario allowed brewers to export their beer into The States, and they also allowed brewers to make near beers with 2% or less alcohol by volume. Labatt

◀ **A NATURAL BUSINESSMAN** Labatt's founding father, John, was a brewmaster, town councillor, and farmer.

▶ **PREMIUM QUALITY** Introduced in 1954, Blue Star was awarded the Gold Medal of Leadership in Munich. A popular Newfoundland lager, Blue Star is aged for smoothness and delivers a full, smooth body. Blue Star has a slight fruity aroma that is balanced by the unique taste and aroma characteristics from selected Hallertau hops.

▼ **LABATT IS KIDNAPPED** Ransom letter sent to Hugh Labatt by Canadian gangster, Three-fingered Abe, demanding a sizable ransom payout.

▲ **SINCE 1828** The first Labatt Brewhouse built in 1828.

survived by producing beer for export, and by introducing two "temperance ales" which had less than 2% alcohol.

They were also clever in finding ways to keep brand recognition alive, despite the fact advertising alcoholic beverages was restricted during prohibition. Labatt effectively advertised itself by supporting community service programs as well as a number of social causes, which strengthened its ties with the public and helped to sustain solid product sales. By the end of Prohibition in 1927, Labatt's competitors had dropped from well over 50 to a mere 14, strengthening their market position.

Not too long later, the family made national headlines, but not for their beer. In 1934, an infamous Canadian gangster named Three-fingered Abe kidnapped John S. Labatt, demanding 150K, a hefty sum at the time. He was held captive for days, and released at Toronto's Royal York Hotel. Thereafter, he became something of a recluse, and Hugh MacKenzie emerged as an important figure in the company's history.

MacKenzie was a savvy businessman, who led the company with grace and precision through The Depression, World War II, and into a period of rapid expansion. They were running full-colour ads everywhere imaginable, sponsoring radio shows, and generally filling the eyes and ears of Canadians with their products.

When they bought out their first brewery in 1946 (Copland Brewery in Toronto), it marked the beginning of their stride towards national domination of the Canadian beer market. By 1952 they were setting up Labatt Breweries in other provinces, and embarked on "a period of rapid expansion with the ultimate goal of becoming Canada's national brewer."

The company itself calls their 1962 acquisition of Bavarian Brewing in St. John's a major milestone in their rise to becoming Canada's biggest national brewer. During this period of growth, Labatt 50 became the country's bestselling brand of beer. In 1951, Labatt launched its Pilsener Lager, setting the trend for lager beers in Canada. Labatt was also the first Canadian brewer to introduce a light beer, the first brewery to do a twist-off cap, and they were also the first Canadian brewer to form an international licensing agreement with a major U.S. brewery.

Pilsener Lager was eventually dubbed "Labatt Blue" in Manitoba, on account of the beer's blue label, and for the company's support of "The Blue Bombers" (Winnipeg's Canadian Football League franchise). The nickname stuck, and became the official name of Labatt Blue, their flagship beer that was for many years Canada's market-leading beer.

In 1995, Labatt was acquired by Interbrew, which in 2004 merged with AmBev, to create InBev, which in 2008 acquired Anheuser-Busch. Anheuser-Busch InBev is now the global leader in beer brands and sales. They own a lot of the beer companies you know: Budweiser, Labatt, Corona, Stella Artois, Beck's, Hoegaarden, Michelob, and more.

Blue Star

ABV & TYPE: 5% Lager

APPEARANCE: Very pale hay-bale colour. See-through. No head or lace

AROMA: Slightly and vaguely floral, but mainly fresh apples and a sweet, grainy whiff

TEXTURE: As its beer label says, it is "aged for smoothness" and is certainly a smooth beer for a bender. Moderate carbonation

TASTE: The distinct Blue Star taste is said to come from its select Hallertau hops, not that this easy-drinking lager is at all a hoppy beer. It's bready and metallic mostly, with some indistinct orchard-fruit notes

BEHIND THE BEER: Blue Star was initially created by Newfoundland's Bavarian Brewing (1932-1962). It was their name-maker the year it was born, as it won a Munich Gold Medal in Germany, in 1954.

Blue Star was so popular in Newfoundland, that when Labatt bought out Bavarian they continued to brew it here, and only here, because it was in such high demand.

At this time, Blue Star was neck and neck with Black Horse as the go-to beer for a younger generation, a demographic that bought plenty of beer, so they had to find a way to stay competitive. To do so, they played up the fact Black Horse wasn't born of Newfoundland the way Blue Star was (Dawes in Montreal created Black Horse).

A series of patriotic ads with a sense of humour about local culture and language played up and branded Blue Star's local heritage with lines like "The Ultimate Newfoundland Beer, for Newfoundlanders, by Newfoundlanders" and "The Shining Star of the Granite Planet." For years, radio ads used humour, wit, and the Newfoundland dialect to win over a new generation of beer drinkers. The marketing strategy worked, the ad campaign won major awards, and the brand's share more than doubled, without eating into sales of Labatt's other products.

Blue Star is as beloved now as it ever was. The proof is in the sales: Blue Star is the top-selling local brand of beer in Newfoundland at the NLC.

Jockey Club

ABV & TYPE: 5% Lager

APPEARANCE: Straw-coloured with a short-lived bubbly head

AROMA: Peppery with a slice of something sweet. Some grassy and floral hints

TEXTURE: Crisp and goes foamy-smooth in the backend of the sip. Moderate body with a higher than average carbonation, and a fairly dry finish

TASTE: Taste of metals and pepper with some woody spicing and slightlybiscuity malt. Legend goes there's hints of sparkling wine in here. Or so it's implied in old ads. Slightly sweet malts with some roundly hoppy bitterness

BEHIND THE BEER: Jockey Club was created by a renowned German brew-master named Hans Schneider, who is generally considered the most influential brewer in the history of brewing in Newfoundland. Schneider was cherry picked from Germany, and brought to Newfoundland to revolutionize brewing on the island in the years just after prohibition, when people started pumping out beer again.

He came up with the recipe for Jockey Club in his tiny apartment above Bavarian Brewing on Leslie Street. It's considered his best creation, and Labatt acquired rights to Jockey Club when it bought out Bavarian Brewing in 1962. Bavarian used to advertise this beer as "The Champagne of Beers." Some say there's hints of sparkling wine in the taste.

As it turns out though, had Jockey Club been retired with the 1962 buyout of Bavarian Brewing, Schneider's prized Jockey would have at least lived on in the ethos of a Nova Scotian craft brewery. Spindrift's co-founder Andrew Bell is the grandson of Charles R. Bell, a one-time director of Bavarian Brewing, and a great grandson of Albert E. Hickman who founded Bavarian Brewing. Spindrift pay homage to Bavarian's and Schneider's style of brewing with their signature beer, Spindrift Coastal Lager, which you can find at the NLC, and many restaurants. Ultimately, Jockey Club is what a slogan of its past calls it: "An Honest Uncomplicated Brew, the Original Bavarian Style." Today's labels say "True Newfoundland Character," presumably a relic from the time in the 1990s when all of Newfoundland's local beers fought for the glory of being deemed The Truest Brew of Newfoundland. Jockey is brewed here and only here by Labatt.

"THE CHAMPAGNE OF BEERS"
Jockey Club when it was made by Bavarian, c. 1960s. [Image courtesy of Chris Conway]

ST. JOHN'S BEER HALL Mill Street has brewed a lot of temporarily available and locally themed beers like Dark NL, RDF, Sazzy Sailor, Nan's Banana Bread, and even one called Touton Topper, a "molasses imperial stout."

MILL STREET BREWERY

2016, ST. JOHN'S

Mill Street Brewery does not brew any permanently available local beers, but they do brew small-batch beers exclusive to here, at their open-concept brewpub on the harbourfront of our capital city. These include regular offerings and past temporary small-batch brews like Touton Topper (imperial stout), RDF (Hefe), #DarkNL (Schawrtzbier), Nan's Banana Bread (Dunkelweissen), and an IPA (Town House Red) based on a song by MusicNL's 2017 Rising Star of the Year winner, Town House.

Upon opening shop in St. John's, Mill Street made it clear that crafting locally inspired, small batch (ie temporarily available) beers would be a primary goal of theirs.

"We want to brew innovative, small batch beers exclusively for the enjoyment of local beer lovers. We want to become part of the St. John's community. This is a fantastic opportunity for us to showcase our family of beers and brew seasonal specialty beers that will be a constant source of new local flavours and experiences for our fans in St. John's."

As an homage to generations of Newfoundland sailors, Mill Street's first local brew was the Longshore Porter, which they called "a fitting tribute to the Longshoremen who built St. John's into the great port town it has long been."

Longshore Porter was Mill Street's first-ever batch-brewed beer made in Atlantic Canada. There have been several since, including a collaboration brew with Port Rexton Brewery. The two brewmakers joined forces to create a Dunkelweizen, which is a darker twist on the Hefeweizen (dunkel means dark in German). The beer was launched at a party with a mac'n'cheese bar. Port Rexton launched their Chasing Sun NEIPA at this same event. Mill Street often have beer events like this, with details on their website.

Mill Street Brewery was founded in December 2002 in Toronto, and named after its original location at 55 Mill Street in the historic Distillery District. Their first ever beer remains their most popular: Mill Street Organic, a lager that was the first ever organic

▲ **RAISING THE BAR** Steve Abrams co-founded Mill Street Brewery in 2002. Their first beer was Original Organic Lager. It was also the first organic beer ever brewed in Ontario.

▲ **A NATIONAL CHAIN WITH LOCAL FLAVOUR** Mill Street makes seasonal beers available in St. John's only. Like their "Town House Red IPA" that was based on a song by the award-wining St. Johns band, Town House.

beer brewed in Ontario. Their other flagship beers include Tankhouse Ale, 100th Meridian Amber Lager, and Cobblestone Stout.

They make roughly 60 beers at this point, if you include seasonals, and have won 100+ awards, including Canadian Brewery of the Year at the Canadian Brewing Awards in 2007, 2008, and 2009.

Mill Street Brewpub in St. John's was their 5th Brewpub in Canada, and their first venture outside of Ontario. They share their space with The Bier Markt, and the partnership was the first of its kind in Canada for these two chains. Patrons can choose between Mill Street's beer offerings (including some local-only offerings) or they can peruse Bier Markt's unrivalled selection of beers.

In terms of food, Mill Street's beer spills over into its brewpub's menu as well, with items like Belgian Pale Ale & Mussel soup, Spent Grain Brewer's Bread, or Beer-Brined Fried Chicken.

MOLSON

1962, ST. JOHN'S

MOLSON Coors

Molson marched into Newfoundland's brewery scene in 1962, the same year they bought out Newfoundland Brewery. Today, Molson brews three historically local beers here and only here: Black Horse, Dominion Ale, and India Beer.

Molson Brewery began its operation 176 years before setting foot on Newfoundland soil, in 1786, making it the country's oldest brewery. John Molson founded his brewery on the banks of the St. Lawrence River in Montreal, and told his diary, "My beer has been universally well-liked beyond my most sanguine expectations."

To make that well-received beer, Molson developed his own strain of yeast for brewing. If that sounds impressive, he also built Canada's first steamboat. The *Accommodation*, which grew into a fleet of steamboats used to transport people and goods between Quebec and Ontario. He also started a distillery, theatre, and hotel. Molson and his sons also founded a bank which would later merge with Bank of Montreal. When he died in 1836, he was involved in building Canada's railway system (he put up a quarter of its cost).

His life story is a lot more impressive given that Molson was only 18 when he left England for Canada in 1782. He started working at Thomas Loyd brewery immediately upon arrival in Montreal, and a mere two years later, he purchased it in an auction with money he inherited from his parents.

At the ripe young age of 20, Molson read the market: the retail prices for wine, rum, and port were rising beyond what people wanted to pay, and a steady stream of incoming English and Irish immigrants wanted beer more than wine and rum anyway.

The delay between his buying the brewery, and officially opening it as Molson Brewery was on account of his trip back across the sea to England, so he could buy some modern equipment, and stockpile ingredients, including seeds he gave to neighbouring Montreal farmers who grew them for him, so his Malt needs were set.

Six weeks after setting up in 1786, he was selling Molson beer, 5 cents a bottle, and people were literally drinking it up. The brewery remained a family run business, and John's

◀ **BEYOND EXPECTATIONS** John Molson founded his brewery on the banks of the St. Lawrence River in Montreal, and told his diary, "My beer has been universally well-liked beyond my most sanguine expectations."

▶ **SINCE 1786** Molson Brewery, c. 1855. The Molson Brewery is the oldest brewery in North America and continues to produce beer on this site.

▶ **1924 ADVERTISMENT** Fifty six years ago when Sir John A. Macdonald was first premier of the Dominion of Canada in 1867, Molson's Ale was then 81 years old!

MOLSON

Established 1786

The Ale your great-g

◀ **PREPARED FOR DELIVERY** Molson Export was Molson's bread and butter before Molson Canadian came along in 1959.

▶ **HORSE-DRAWN DELIVERY** Molson's Brewery used horses for its beer deliveries in the early days.

great-grandson Herbert Molson, inspired by imported beers, created the legendary Molson Export in 1903. Its best known beer, Molson Canadian, hit shelves in 1959, gaining them much popularity just three years before the brewery showed up in Newfoundland.

Business was good for Molson Brewery in the 1950s, but other Canadian breweries were consolidating their resources in an attempt to compete with them. Proactively, Molson decided the route to rise to the status of untouchable giant in Canadian brewing was to expand significantly and have a brewery operating in each province, so as to really flood the market with their beers. They started this in motion by building a brewery in Toronto. The expansion effort saw their earnings more than double.

At this point, they knew Molson Brewery was approaching the limits of their profitability, and saw acquisitions, or corporate takeovers of other breweries and brands as a way to keep the profits soaring. In 1958, they began acquiring other breweries, starting with Sick's Brewery. They bought out Fort Garry Brewery in Winnipeg in 1959, and next up, they hit Newfoundland by buying Newfoundland Brewery in 1962 (and along with it, rights to India Beer).

Their 1989 merger with Carling O'Keefe made Molson the largest brewery in Canada, and the fifth largest in the world. During that merger they acquired rights to two other long-standing local beers, Black Horse and Dominion Ale. The growth didn't stop there. In 2005, Molson merged with US-based Coors to form Molson Coors Brewing Company.

A series of other mergers has made Molson Coors the world's third largest brewer. In addition to their own well-known beers, Molson Coors now own well-known companies as small as Granville Island Brewing and Creemore Springs, to ones as large as Rickards, and hold the marketing and selling rights for Heineken and Miller in Canada. Seventh generation Molson family members continue to be involved with the company.

Black Horse

ABV & TYPE: 5% Lager

APPEARANCE: Clear straw yellow, with a little head and soda-like bubbling

AROMA: Hay, celery, and sweet grains, with some vaguely floral and spicy hops

TEXTURE: Clean, crisp, and pretty easy drinking, with ample carbonation: a texture to make the tongue tingle for more

TASTE: Primarily an undescript sweetness from the malt, and a little bit of smoothed-over bitterness from the hops. Hints of granny smith apple, with a clean mineral finish. Its brewer says "a cool fermentation brings out all the refreshment a beer can give. The specially selected traditional hops provide a crisp cleansing hop bitter finish."

BEHIND THE BEER: Of all the beer exclusively sold in Newfoundland, Black Horse has the most storied history, and the most roundabout trip to becoming a beer exclusive to here.

The journey involved Black Horse galloping to Newfoundland, and hiding out here long after it was discontinued across mainland Canada. Black Horse actually started out as a small craft beer out of small-town Quebec all the way back in 1826. The Black Horse on its logo is the breed of horse (Percheron noir) that was used to run deliveries around small towns in Quebec at the time.

Black Horse Ale was one of the most popular beers in Quebec for decades, but competition was getting tough in the early years of the 1900s. At this time, many Quebec breweries were spending considerable money on competing with each other, including Dawes, Dow, Boswell, and Molson. In 1909, over a dozen of them decided to band together and become "National Breweries LTD" in an attempt to avoid actively competing with each other. In 1952, a conglomerate company called Canadian Breweries bought out National Breweries, and that's how a national brewer, Canadian Breweries, came to own Dawe's Black Horse brand.

In time, Canadian Breweries began retiring many of National Breweries' brands (now attributed to Dow Brewery) up in Canada, including Black Horse Ale. So how did Black Horse end up here? Well, Canadian Breweries LTD was sold to cigarette maker Rothman's Pall Mall, who renamed the company to Carling-O'Keefe.

Carling-OKeefe was one of the country's top 3 breweries, and they'd been buying up independent breweries around the country, and this included their 1962 purchase of Bennett Brewing in St. John's. Carling-Okeefe used this NL-based plant to produce and sell their newly acquired Black Horse brand in Newfoundland in 1968 or 1969. And we liked it. A lot. There was a demand for it, a thirst so strong Carling O'Keefe kept making it here, and only here, after it was discontinued everywhere else in Canada, including its province of origin, Quebec.

Molson bought out Carling-O'Keefe in 1989, and closed down Bennett Brewing's plant, but with Black Horse performing so well in the local market, Molson also decided to keep brewing the stuff, and still do to this day. In fact, they have sunk millions of dollars into advertising it as part of our history, so the beer would conjure the same sense of nostalgia and ownership as does the province's other 4 longest-standing beers: Dominion Ale, India Beer, Blue Star, and Jockey Club.

You'll note that Black Horse still has its own Black Horse cap while all other Molson beers on the island simply say Molson. And if you take a look at the new label (new as of 2010), the black horse on it has a shadow in the shape of our province, atop its hind legs.

"In addition, there is the outline of a 'BOB 21' beer bottle between its hind legs," says Molson's Jason Hull. BOB 21s are the uniquely sized bottle used by breweries in Newfoundland. "Our goal was to remove the horse in the previous design and return it to the traditional horse with the 2 additions. Mostly to pay respect to the province and have a bit of fun."

Its original recipe has been changed, and you can track these changes on various Black Horse labels through the years, Black Horse ALE became a vaguely labelled Black Horse BEER in the 1970s, and is today labelled as a "Premium Lager." This complete change of style was an attempt to bend Black Horse to meet popular tastes or trends in the past, when demand for easier drinking lagers piqued, and, here in NL, lingered. It is a legendary breed of beer for sure, but its pedigree has been altered along its journey from a

microbrew ale out of Quebec to a macro-brew lager out of Newfoundland.

Its transformation hasn't hurt sales. Black Horse remains a top-3 bestselling local beer at the NLC, and, among many beer snobs, it's the favourite of NL's Big Five (Black Horse, India, Blue Star, Jockey, and Dominion).

Dominion Ale

ABV & TYPE: 5% Lager

APPEARANCE: Pale gold with a bit of head and lacing. Some claim to see a unique green sheen

AROMA: Smells a fair bit like apple cider, actually, with sweet notes of Bazooka Joe bubble gum. Faintly floral with some toffee and nectarines with some vaguely floral and spicy hops

TEXTURE: Well-carbonated and thin, with a dry finish. There's a uniquely foamy smoothness

TASTE: Dominion's unique taste feels a bit like Black Horse cut with a nip of cider. The beer is marked with a very unique apple tang, and a mild floral-peppery hop situation. The tang makes the beer distinct, and the bitterness through the whole sip makes you want another sip. Some hay here too

BEHIND THE BEER: Dominion Ale has the distinction of being the sole surviving creation of Bennett Brewing Company—Bennett was the province's longest-running brewery ever: it operated independently from 1827-1962.

The beer was born in the years after prohibition, when Bennett was allowed to start brewing real beers again. Dominion Ale emerged as a local favourite, and was dubbed "the old smoothie with the hearty flavour."

Old ads for this beer during its heyday in the 50s and 60s positioned it as a manly man's beer, before thankfully shifting towards a focus on the beer's uniqueness, with slogans like "Enjoy a Dominion Ale. You'll know you're having one."

We'll never quite know what they meant by that though. The "Ale" in the title "Dominion Ale" is a relic. Dominion has been a lager since at least the mid-seventies. So until you find an old bottle in nan's attic somewhere, you'll never really know what Dominion Ale tasted like in its original recipe.

To this day, Dominion Ale bottles still feature Bennett Brewing's logo on their boxes and labels as an homage to Bennett's homegrown heritage, and cultural relevance in the 1800s and 1900s. In fact, there was a campaign going for a while where Molson printed local stories on labels on the bottles, to, in part, remind us that Dominion is the ultimate, longest standing, all-local beer.

Today, in corner stores across the island, Dominion Ale stands strong as a solid offering of something with character that shines for its class. More than one Molson employee brewing in Newfoundland has declared Dominion Ale their personal favourite Molson product.

India Beer

ABV & TYPE: 5% Lager

APPEARANCE: Pale, gold, and clear with some head and a wee bit of lace

AROMA: Primarily a malt grain smell, and fairly bready. There's some creamed corn, hay, and something fruity in the way of diced pears. The hops are vaguely floral in the nose

TEXTURE: Light, smooth, and thirst-quenching with a nice acidic snap at the back-end of your sip. There's some substance here, but not enough to slow you down too much on a weekend bender. India has a dry finish with a mild hop aftertaste

TASTE: A well-balanced beer with nothing wild enough going on to offend any palate, but more substance than most macrobrews. Taste is primarily copper and cut apples with some breadiness alongside its slightly spicy hops

BEHIND THE BEER: India Beer was initially created and brewed by a local microbrewery called Newfoundland Brewery Limited (1893-1962), and it remains the sole beer from that legendary local brewery that is still brewed today.

According to one retired Molson employee "India Beer was a 20% brand, and it was a Gold Medal Winner at an international beer tasting show in the 1970s."

Contrary to popular belief, India Beer is not an India Pale Ale, it is a lager. Newfoundland Brewery LTD made both an India Beer and an India Pale Ale that once coexisted: India Beer was a lighter, easier version of the fiercer India Pale Ale.

Also, contrary to folkore, India is not "named after the dog on the label." The proof is in the history of the labels. India Beer existed for a very long time before that Newfoundland dog appeared on its label, so, if the dog's name really is India, it's more likely the dog was named after the beer than the opposite.

There's also the expression, "Get dat Indi-ya," i.e., get that into you, which has nothing to do with the origins of its name so much as locals' enthusiasm for drinking the stuff. India Beer has been around for more than 100 years, and is consistently voted by readers of *The Overcast* as the "Best Local Macrobrew."

It's a real favourite among blossoming beer connoisseurs and students who love beer but can't justify the double-digit price tags on all those imported craft beer bombers at the NLC. Plenty of beer lovers call it Molson's best offering.

According to Sales Manager Jason Hull, "People like that it's only brewed here.

It's been around for about 130 years. It's a very, very solid brand, and it's been on the rise for the past number of years." More than 1 in 100 beer in Newfoundland at any given moment is an India, and you can find the stuff on tap in select pubs and restaurants around the island.

THE OLD BLUE INDIA LABEL c. 1970s. India Beer is the only remaining beer still in production from the Newfoundland Brewery's range of products.

PUTTING NEGLECTED LOCAL APPLE TREES TO WORK

The revitalization of rural communities in Newfoundland has come down to entrepreneurs like Chris Adams and Marc Poirier seeing and seizing opportunities. The duo has turned forgotten-about apple trees into the province's only orchard, and, their supply for our first cidery.

NEWFOUNDLAND CIDER COMPANY

2017, MILTON

The demand for cider in Newfoundland came seemingly out of nowhere in the 2010s, perhaps because ciders were poorly known and poorly marketed here, not to mention the slim pickings available to us. For a while there, it was Strongbow or nothing.

Marc Poirier and Chris Adams, the force behind our province's first cidery, had been homebrewing cider long before the NLC starting giving more shelf space to the stuff. When Chris moved to Ireland for a while, he happily discovered that ciders were a much more common drink there than in Newfoundland, and he was able to try a lot of great examples of ciders, in all their variations, from dry to sweet, and smoky and strange.

Upon moving back home to Newfoundland, he couldn't help but notice all the unused apple trees in his hometown of Milton. Milton's unique geography creates a protected valley that apple trees do quite well in. Locals discovered this and planted them amply many years ago, but the trees were producing more than anyone was eating, so the apples dropped to the ground, rolled around, and laid the seeds for new apple trees. This created a kingdom of apples for the Newfoundland Cider Company to put to use in their cidery.

There are nearly eight thousand species of apples, and Poirier and Adams didn't plant the ones they started making cider from, so they weren't even sure what they were making their first batches with. While there's a nice air of mystery in their early bottles on account of this, the duo started their own orchard in Milton, in part to know what kinds of apples they're working with. It's province's first official orchard.

Newfoundland Cider Company built their cidery and taproom in Milton in the spring of 2017. They make small batches of different types of ciders to offer the full range of their drink of choice from dry to sweet, still to sparkling, straight-up to botanical, and more. They launched with three core, permanent offerings listed below. Their plan upon

A TEAM EFFORT
The Newfoundland Cider Company team.

launching was to stay small, plant some new and different types of apple trees, and expand considerably after 5-6 years of operation.

Prior to their opening, no one was making cider in Newfoundland, with the exception of YellowBelly's occasional small batch offering, or their more regularly available Crooked as Sin cider (of which Chris is a fan), so Marc and Chris set out to raise the stature of cider in our province. The duo is dedicated to making cider the traditional way, as Poirier rightfully points out that the vast majority of ciders available in the province come from breweries that rely on imported ingredients, and breweries that admittedly inject their "ciders" with artificial flavours. Many of these offerings admit that right on the can, like Mad Jack, which are labelled as "apple-flavoured beer" instead of ciders.

Newfoundland Cider Company's story is a classic tale of filling a niche and doing it right: they wanted a steady stream of quality ciders for the people of their province, and looking around their hometown, they had the apples to do it. Poirier was confident there'd be demand for a local cider company because consumption of cider in Newfoundland increased almost fourfold during the 2010s. He also adds that an increasing demand for locally produced products, like a cider, is entirely in-line with trends in our newly booming food and drink industry.

Adams is a horticulturist by trade, and acts as cider maker, while Poirier has a forestry background and is an arborist by trade, so he spends much of his time in the orchard, caring for the trees, and the rest of his time acting as primary business-and-marketing man for the operation.

Milton is at the gateway of the Bonavista peninsula, so it's very well positioned to attract plenty of tourists and baycationers. You can buy their ciders at select NLC locations as well.

Black Lav

ABV & TYPE: 6% Cider

APPEARANCE: Rosy amber colour

AROMA: Dominated by a floral lavender aroma as the head gently dissipates with hints of woodsy blackcurrant

TEXTURE: Medium body and carbonation

TASTE: Semi sweet, with floral and woodsy notes. Finishes with a slightly tart snap that makes you want another sip

BEHIND THE BEER: Black Lav was the first of Newfoundland Cider Company's Botanical series. Botanical ciders marry the natural qualities of a cider to complementary flavours and textures from herbs and flowers. Now that ciders are among North America's fastest growing markets in the food biz, pairing apples with complementary florals is a real trend in the cidery scene, as a way of diversifying offerings, and there are some particularly adventurous botanical ciders out there.

Newfoundland Cider Company make Black Lav by infusing a specially blended cider with locally grown lavender and blackcurrant, and call it "a refreshing cider with floral aromas that will remind you of the height of summer." Fittingly recommended as a perfect companion for a BBQ, Black Lav captures the essence of summer in a bottle.

Forager Barrel Aged Cider

ABV & TYPE: 6% Cider

APPEARANCE: Amber

AROMA: Apple, with hints of whiskey barrel

TEXTURE: Medium body, with light to medium carbonation

TASTE: Dry, crisp, and clean, with undertones of oak and whiskey. Finishes with a gentle tartiness

BEHIND THE BEER: As with wine, aging cider in oak barrels can add desirable body, flavour, and complexity. For their Forager Barrel Aged Cider, Newfoundland Cider Company uses oak whiskey barrels to add something special and distinct to the cider. The whiskey notes wind up defining a lot of what makes this cider unique.

In fact, barrel aging harkens back to how ciders were originally made. Fermenting cider in oak was common before the advent of stainless steel tanks, and to this day in Spain, "Sidra" is served from the enormous oak barrels they were aged in.

Forager Barrel Aged Cider is made from wild apples foraged from along the sea front and forest, Marc Poirier says. "We blend up to 20 different varieties and ferment to dry. Then we let the cider mature through the winter in whiskey barrels before bottle conditioning for another 6 months."

"Each vintage will be slightly different from one year to the next," Poirier adds. "Tastes will vary depending on which wild apple trees we harvest, and what type of whiskey barrels we use." Again, like wine, ciders pair well with food. Forager makes an excellent companion drink for charcuterie, steak, gourmet burgers, or a proper plate of fish and chips.

Old Tilt

ABV & TYPE: 6% Cider

APPEARANCE: Gold in colour

AROMA: Sweet apple notes

TEXTURE: Medium body and carbonation

TASTE: A sweet, fresh tasting cider

BEHIND THE BEER: Old Tilt is named after an old, abandoned, long-forgotten orchard in Milton. The very same place Newfoundland Cider Company established their new orchard.

Old Tilt is made using a blend of apples to conjure up a sweet, medium-bodied cider. It pairs well with a lot of seafood and cheeses like Brie and cheddar. Refreshing on a hot summer day, it works to wash down sausages as well.

FROM BLOSSOM TO BOTTLE Forager Cider is made from wild Newfoundland apples and aged for 2 years in oak whiskey barrels. You can really taste the trace bourbon notes. The Old Tilt is a relatively sweeter cider, barrel aged for three months.

PORT REXTON BREWING

2016, PORT REXTON

Port Rexton Brewing became a very welcome, and immediately adored addition to the Newfoundland craft-beer scene in the summer of 2016. There was such demand for their products that they had to order in two new double-sized fermenters before their first anniversary, to keep up with that demand.

Named after the town they operate out of, Port Rexton Brewing is co-owned by a married couple, Alicia MacDonald (Toronto-born) and Sonja Mills (Clarenville-born), who met "hesitantly, over a casual beer through a mutual friend's insistence."

Were it not for their insistent friend, we wouldn't have had our fourth commercial microbrewery here in NL. Port Rexton was the first microbrewery to open in our province in 8 years, and it's no coincidence that since their opening in 2016, 8 other micro-breweries quickly applied for licensing. Their success, and quality beer, was literally inspiring for many others.

Over the course of that casual drink, what Alicia and Sonja found they had in common was a passion for craft beer. And we're talking true passion here: this couple has been known to ski to pubs on storm days, and their road trips "always include at least one microbrewery stop. We even built a craft-beer bar for our craft-beer themed wedding. No joke."

The two gathered a lot of experience by living in Nova Scotia during its craft brewery movement. "Initially, we frequented craft-beer bars in Halifax, visited new microbreweries as they opened, and were members of the Ladies Beer League. As the craft-beer scene evolved in Nova Scotia, we attended many unique and educational events and festivals." Before too long, Alicia was apprenticing and brewing.

In doing so, they established many beneficial contacts and working relationships to help them get their start here in Port Rexton. The duo are drawn to beer as a product because

ALWAYS COOKIN' UP SOMETHING In addition to their core beers, Port Rexton keeps offerings fresh with various one-off small batches or recurring seasonals like their Nor-Easter (Partridgeberry Porter), Sweater Weather (Double IPA), Mr. Wheaty Pants (Wheat Ale), and their Saison, Mixed Opportunity.

"craft beer is not only a social product, but a product of science and art." They marry that science-art balance to perfection and make true, truly delicious, cut-no-corners craft beer.

"As a social industry," they say, "beer, and particularly good beer, brings people together." They're right about that. On a visit to the brewery in its first month of operation, the author of this article couldn't find a seat to sit in, as the brewery was that packed with people from all over the world. A kind crowd of folks from all over Canada made room at their table, and we got to talking about our favourite craft breweries throughout the country (and how well Port Rexton's beer was standing up to them).

Sonja and Alicia operate out of a converted schoolhouse-turned community-centre in their stunningly quaint namesake town of Port Rexton, where they got engaged and married. The space is open concept with a taproom where you can sit and order pints, taster flights, or takeaway growlers. In addition to their 4 core beers, they also offer an ever-changing small-batch series you can try at their taproom. They also have a retail space in St. John's now, with limited hours. They're selling their beer at 286 Torbay Road.

Their small-batch runs are a treat to try because of their short-lived nature: they only make a few kegs of these each time, so, you gotta get 'em while you can, and what better way to lure repeat customers and UnTappd app addicts to your brewhouse? These small-batch beers have included things like a Witbier called Mr. Wheaty Pants, "Rose Hip Wonder" (a specialty ale infused with rose hips), and the cleverly named We Ryes Again (a rye ale). Big Cod Mountain Ridge was an ale whose ingredients were 100% sourced from Atlantic Canada.

When they opened, they were the only local brewer offering a bold West Coast Style IPA, and their T-Rex Porter was the only constantly available craft porter on the island (Storm's is seasonal). That was on purpose. Gifting the island the things it didn't have was part of their purpose. "We got into this business to create products we would be proud of and could share with other people."

Baycation Blonde Ale

ABV & TYPE: 5.4% Blonde Ale

APPEARANCE: Pale straw-gold, with some true head and lacing

AROMA: A moderately sweet malty aroma, with nice hints of hop spice

TEXTURE: Crisp and clean, super refreshing finish. This is Port Rexton's easy-drinker

TASTE: It's a nice blonde ale that really nails the style and would tickle anyone's fancy for refreshment. Its toasted malty sweetness is something to write home about, and it's balanced nicely by an aromatic-yet-gently spicy hop profile

BEHIND THE BEER: Port Rexton Brewing enjoyed plenty of traffic through their brewery the summer they opened, and sold enough beer to say that Baycation Blonde Ale might be their most popular offering.

They attribute this to the fact that plenty of visitors to Port Rexton are there for the hiking, or they're wandering around the beautiful town's hillsides and coastline, and when they stumble into the taproom, they're parched, The Baycation Blonde Ale happens to be a really refreshing post-hike beer, or day beer. It's not too heavy, as it's brewed to be a crisp refreshing drink.

Plus, a lot of microbreweries opt to have an accessible beer on tap, something solid and satisfying, but something approachable for any craft-beer novices in the pub. Baycation Blonde Ale is a great beer in its own right, but it's also a sort of gateway into the Port Rexton's bolder, more adventurous offerings. "We wanted to offer something that was not too bold on any front, but still had a clean and flavourful taste so it still stood apart from mainstream beers."

They were smart to have such an offering. "A lot of people come to our brewery and ask for our lightest beer, so we wanted an option where it was lighter in colour and easier drinking, but yet gave them a bit more flavour than they're probably typically used to. The IPA and the Porter have bolder flavours, so the Blonde is a nice starting point."

ON TAP

1. POTHOLE SMASH (JANE'S) — PALE ALE & NELSON HOPS — ABV 5.6% IBU 23
2. MIXED OPPORTUNITY — SAISON & BRETT — ABV 6.5% IBU 23
3. CLEAR AS MUD — DUNKELWEISEN - COLLAB: MILL ST — ABV 5.2% IBU 22
4. CHASING SUN — NEIPA — ABV 6.5% IBU 45
5. T-REX PORTER — ABV 5.8% IBU 19
6. HORSE CHOPS — IPA — ABV 6.3% IBU 72
7. NAB BITTER — EXTRA SPECIAL BITTER — ABV 5.5% IBU 30
8. —

Chasing Sun NEIPA

ABV & TYPE: 6% New England Style IPA

APPEARANCE: Bright and hazy

AROMA: Loads of juicy, unique Amarillo hop aromatics, as the beer is heavily dry-hopped

TEXTURE: Medium body and carbonation with a smooth mouthfeel from the oats and wheat

TASTE: Fairly dry with some hop bitterness, but the focus is mostly on the citrus and stone-fruit flavours

BEHIND THE BEER: Nearly a year after the popularity of their west-coast style Horse Chops IPA won over the province (it was voted Best Craft Beer in NL by readers of *The Overcast* in 2016), Port Rexton Brewing launched a second permanently available IPA, Chasing Sun, but this one is a New England style IPA. It as a lower IBU (45 versus 72) than Horse Chops, so, it's less bitter, and that's the point.

NEIPAs are hazy, tropical, less bitter, and relatively smoother spin on IPAs (the haziness is linked to their creamier mouthfeel). A relatively new style of beer, NEIPAs were developed as a reaction to the increasing focus on bitterness of West Coast IPAs. NEIPAs also tend to have a juicy quality that other IPAs do not. All these qualities come from the choice of hops used.

"We fell in love with these New England IPAs from trying a few examples brewed in New Brunswick and Ontario," says Sonja Mills, "and we couldn't wait to develop our own version." To do so, they used a very small amount of bittering hops at first wort, left the rest of their hop additions to the whirlpool, and did a double dry-hop during primary fermentation.

They also used a good deal of oats and wheat in their grain bill to help increase the mouthfeel, as a way to accompany the juicy flavours from the hops. "We also used a Vermont Ale yeast strain that helps further bring out a stone-fruit and citrus character, accompanied by a smooth body."

As for the name, Chasing Sun, it derives from the bright hazy look of the beer, which reminded them of the sun. "We developed this recipe during a late winter when the sun was highly sought after," she jokes.

Gardener's Gose

ABV & TYPE: 6% Cider

APPEARANCE: Hazy yellow

AROMA: Sour citrus notes with hints of coriander, and notes of cilantro. Nice enough to be worn as a perfume

TEXTURE: Thin and highly carbonated

TASTE: This beer is true to its gose style with a slightly tart and salty profile. The coriander really punches through in its taste

BEHIND THE BEER: Gose, pronounced *go-za,* is a style of beer semi-familiar to Germans, but an uncommon offering in the rest of the world. No one else in Newfoundland makes a gose, so Port Rexton's is the only way to sample a style of beer so rare it has gone extinct in the world more than once.

Its unique nature was their inspiration to brew it. "We really strive to offer styles and flavours that are not brewed here to offer variety, and entice people to try new styles."

This beer is a collaboration with the stunning Fishers' Loft Inn, in Port Rexton. Coriander is a big, defining component of a gose. It's basically a substitute for hops as the beer's spice (though some brewer's heavily hop their goses, others don't). So when brewmaster Alicia found a solid supply of locally grown coriander, she knew she wanted to introduce this rare style of beer to their patrons.

"We were really excited to do a collaboration brew with Fishers' Loft. Having their readily available coriander just adds to the local movement this province is becoming known for." They only make this beer in the summer, and you can often find it bottled at Fishers' Loft.

The most distinguishing feature of a gose is saltiness, not something your tongue is accustomed to after a swig of beer, and goses are also known for their tartness. Both the salt and sour notes come from it being fermented with not just yeast, like all beers, but also some lactic bacteria. The brewery embraced the fact that Newfoundland has naturally high levels of sodium in its water. "The Gose style typically has added salt, to encourage the salty profile of the style. We are attempting to replicate this style without adding (too much) salt."

Horse Chops IPA

ABV & TYPE: 6% West Coast Style IPA

APPEARANCE: A gorgeous, glowing, deep golden yellow with a copper hue

AROMA: Loads of tropical fruit and floral aromas from having been generously dry-hopped with mosaic hops

TEXTURE: Medium-bodied and bold, with a dry finish

TASTE: Very west coast. There's a well-balanced melange of citrusy bite and floral brightness in a soft maltiness. All that citrus and floral bouquet lasts right through to the finish. The predominant taste here is bright, beautiful grapefruits, in a bouquet of wildflowers

BEHIND THE BEER: Prior to Port Rexton's Horse Chops IPA, there wasn't a proper West Coast style, tongue-rasping, grape-fruity craft IPA being made on the island. And that was exactly why Port Rexton made this beer one of their core ones.

"We love citrusy IPAs and the province definitely needed one made here." The people of the province appreciated it: it was voted "Best Craft Beer in NL" during The Overcast's People's Choice Awards, 2016.

This is an expressive, memorable, more-ish IPA. It also happens to be the favourite of both Sonja and Alicia—owners of Port Rexton Brewing—who have noticed that visiting beer enthusiasts big on IPAs declare Horse Chops their top pick from Port Rexton's sampler flights. So if you love IPAs, yes, this is a must try.

As for the curious name, it's drawn from one of Newfoundland's many curiously named nooks and crannies (we do have, after all, place names like Joe's Nose,

Cow Head, Dildo, and Blow Me Down). This IPA is named after a point of land at the north side of Trinity Bight that extends east of English Harbour.

Sonja's parents owned a sailboat, and she recalls her father talking about sailing around the rough waters just off the cliffs of Horse Chops. "The name captured us, and being an IPA that has a citrusy and bitter bight, it seemed a proper thing to name it from a place in Trinity Bight."

T-Rex Porter

ABV & TYPE: 6.5% Porter

APPEARANCE: An intense, deep brown

AROMA: A mellow roasted aroma, with hints of chocolate

TEXTURE: A robust beer with a medium body

TASTE: Nice, biscuit roasted malt flavours of chocolate, coffee, cola, and caramel build a medium sweet body that finishes rich in malty dryness

BEHIND THE BEER: Big and balanced, this won "Best Local Beer" in *The Overcast*'s 2017 people's Choice Awards, and they

figure that's because it's a "nice roasty dark beer that is easily enjoyed in the evening," so it tends to be what all their evening visitors order.

In settling on their core beers, Port Rexton knew they wanted "a nice roasted dark beer" and it came down to choosing between an oatmeal stout, or robust porter. "We were really pleased with how our porter had been turning out, and we personally love porters as well. Besides, we live in Port Rexton not Stout Rexton! It's obvious we needed a Porter as a flagship!"

Its fabulous name, T-Rex Porter, came from the history of their building. It was a schoolhouse for many years, and a community centre for many years after that. "When our building was a school, Mr. Thomas Rex was the principal and a very well-respected teacher and community leader. When we were working on the building we came across an old Fire Order that showed the actual name of the community centre was the T. Rex Community Centre. Right away we wanted to name our beer after this well-respected person in Port Rexton. Plus it's a big bold beer, which made T-Rex a fitting name for those who may not know the history."

A lot of casual beer drinkers seem wary of the dark appearance of porters, but needn't be. "One can only guess why people are afraid of the dark! Perhaps because the deep dark appearance is just so different than the light colour of what many are used to, so it makes people fear the unknown? What we do notice is that many people associate dark beer with Guinness' Stout and yet our porter is very different with its sweeter roastiness. After a month of having the taproom open, we found that many patrons who were initially 'afraid of the dark' tried our porter ended up really enjoying this style."

QUIDI VIDI BREWING

1996, QUIDI VIDI VILLAGE

Quidi Vidi Brewing started selling their beer in the summer of 1996, making them the only craft brewery in St. John's at the time, and they were neck and neck with Storm as the first local microbreweries to sell beer in Newfoundland in decades.

This brewery was founded by two local Engineers named David—David Rees and David Fong—and it wasn't their first venture together. In 1985, they formed a firm called RDS Engineering, which landed several big contracts for the Hibernia Oil Rig.

As people in their line of business tend to do, they travelled a lot, and on their travels, they picked up a taste for the local craft beers being made in the various cities they visited. Not only were the beers good, they couldn't help notice business was good for these breweries too. Entrepreneurial light bulbs went off.

The microbrewery scene in North America was enjoying serious growth in the 1990s, and they wanted in on it, so they used their earnings from those Hibernia gigs and opened a brewery in Quidi Vidi Village, to provide the people of Newfoundland with an alternative to the macrobrewery beers they were accustomed to.

They set the brewery up in a space that used to be Cabot Seafood's Plant, and their brewery could not be located in a more picturesque location: Quidi Vidi is a quaint fishing village 10 minutes from downtown St. John's, with a 360-degree view of everything that makes Newfoundland the kind of place people want to visit.

Its co-founding partners put their engineering skills to work and converted the seafood plant into what is today Newfoundland's biggest microbrewery. Despite the building's quaint heritage and location, the company houses an ultra-modern facility and state-of-the-art brewery. It also has a fabulous venue space rented by the public year-round for various events like wedding receptions, Christmas parties, and community affairs.

There are 108 chemicals approved by the Canadian Food and Drug Administration for

QUIDI VIDI IS REDEFINING ITSELF IN 2018 Pictured above are Quidi Vidi's well-known core offerings. As of 2018, fans can get used to a lot more small batch and seasonal offerings out of their newly renovated space. Among their first new offerings was a local crab apple saison.

use in beer, but Quidi Vidi brewery prides itself on using only water, malt, hops, and yeast, hence the adoption of their slogan, "Beer the Way it Should Be." One of the brewery's operating mottos is that they make beer the way it was made over 30 years ago, before big commercial breweries introduced quality-compromising, cost-savings measures into the brewing equation.

Their focus is to produce "quality beers for the mainstream," and it's working. You can find Quidi Vidi basically anywhere beer is sold in the province, including on tap in most bars and restaurants. Their ability to compete in a market dominated by international beer giants like Molson, Labatt, and Guiness is impressive and

commendable, and speaks not just to the quality of the beer, but to their clever marketing prowess.

Quidi Vidi Brewing has been very clever in reading their market. There is a small population here in Newfoundland, and the craft-beer craze only started catching on here a decade or more after they opened, placing them well ahead of the curve. To grow and prosper, they had to balance catering to traditional NL demands for easy-drinking light lagers, while simultaneously—with beers like 1892—providing the craft beer crowd with more adventurous, complex beers. In other words, they've never boxed themselves in. They read the room and offered up a beer for everyone.

They get most expressive with their seasonal beers. As of 2018, we can expect to see more of that. The Brewery has renovated its space, and they've begun offering stunning new small-batch and seasonal beers.

If the story of an engineer turned local beer kingpin sounds surprising, it shouldn't. Dave Fong's love of beer dates back to the early days of his engineering degree, when he was secretly and discreetly brewing homebrew beer in a janitor's closet at his residence at MUN. One weekend, Dave went home to Carbonear for the weekend, and the janitor, who agreed to look after the beer for the weekend, ended up drinking a bunch of the beer, and got so sloppy drunk on campus that campus police picked him up. He ratted Fong out, and Fong's resulting boot from residence marked the start of an epic career in beer!

1892

ABV & TYPE: 5% Ale

APPEARANCE: Opaque, and the colour of a sunset trapped in a funky amber ring. There's a bright orange sheen making it a unique-looking beer—a true downtownie could ID an 1892 on the bar at The Ship just by looking at it. It gives more head than most Quidi Vidi beers, and leaves some lingering lace

AROMA: A clear waft of caramel with some earthiness and herbaceous grass. Very bready too. Nice, and different

TEXTURE: Soft, velvety, and pretty thick: a truly satisfying mouth feel and medium body. It goes easy on carbonation, and has a befitting grassy bitterness in the finish

TASTE: The elegance of the honeyed caramel off the malt really stands out, and makes it more-ish. It's a hearty ale, there's some oatmeal and burnt crème, and the pronounced caramel is more dry than sweet. There's some dark fruit, maybe raisin. The sweetness of the malt is winning the battle over the hops here, but the very distinct and mildly spicy hops are what make the beer's sensational finish. There's fresh bread punching through the beer's complex nature, as a Belgian-esque fermentation flavour

BEHIND THE BEER: 1892 was Quidi Vidi Brewery's first creation. No one was selling craft beer here in the late 1990s, so 1892 was born to grant Newfoundlanders easy access to a substantial, unique ale.

They moved an impressive 48,000 cases in the first year, which is not bad for a start-up that launched a decade ahead of Canada's craft-beer craze, in a province known to favour light lagers. Increasing sales of 1892 was proof a demand for craft ales existed here.

The beer's title, 1892, commemorates the year of the Great Fire in St. John's; the fire that burned the town and its 1500 buildings to the ground. The fire is said to have been caused by a man smoking a pipe on Freshwater Road who accidentally caught a pile of hay on fire. There wasn't enough water around to put it out, so the man cost the city over ten million in damages, and left 11,000 people homeless.

The beer aims to revive the brewing tradition of pre-confederation Newfoundland by following a popular local recipe for brown ale from the 1890s. To do so, they use malt and hop varieties that would have been imported to St. John's in the 1890s—malt from the UK, and hops from the Czech Republic—so it legitimately emulates what beer may have tasted like in St. John's in 1892.

Demand for this truly unique beer has kept it in their wheelhouse since day one. It first hit the market over 20 years ago, and remains the brewery's second-bestseller. For its utterly unique flavour profile, it's a true beer enthusiast's pick from Quidi Vidi's catalogue, and one that is "enjoyed by those who prefer European-style beers with substantial flavour."

You could consider it the perfect gateway beer into craft beer: it's different, very unique, and yet nothing wild enough to scare off whomever you're trying to convert into a micro lover. It's opulent yet not too compact for those who like an accessible beer.

British IPA

ABV & TYPE: 5.7% British Style IPA

APPEARANCE: Pours golden with hues of orange amber

AROMA: Predominantly citrus and sweet malt in the nose, with floral undertones

TEXTURE: It's creamy for an IPA, which works well with the crisp pop and effervescent carbonation. The beer is relatively light and refreshing, as is the Quidi Vidi way, with pleasant acidity, a medium body, and a nice smooth finish

TASTE: The hops connote more piney, resinous, floral tastes on the tongue than citrus ones; most of the beer's citrus notes come from the smell. The citrus that is here is orange, and there's hints of hay. There are some zippy copper tastes here, balanced with the graham cracker and toffee from the malt, and complemented by some herbaceous undertones. It is politely bitter at the finish

BEHIND THE BEER: As it says right on the name of the beer, this is a *British IPA*, an old-world one, not one of those hop-heavy, tongue-rasping, uber-expressive "west coast IPAs" that dominate the markets lately. It is, as Quidi Vidi is known for, an accessible and clean beer. It's not at all over-powering for avid ale drinkers, and it's a good gateway into IPAs for the craft beer newbie.

The beer sells quite well on tap in St. John's 'hop-ing' new food scene, if you catch the pun. "We sell just as much IPA on tap as we do in bottle, which is higher than our other brands. It's a pint beer for sure." The Trans Canada Beer Blog calls British IPA "one of the best commercial beers brewed in Newfoundland ever."

At the time of its release, there wasn't much here on the island in the way of IPAs, so it was created to diversify local craft-beer offerings. It started out as a seasonal that stuck around, perhaps because it won the 2012 Gold Medal at the World Beer Championships in Chicago, who praised its "crisp, frothy, medium body and nicely astringent, honeyed citrus and mineral hop finish. A very nice food beer that really nails the British IPA hop profile."

Speaking of food pairings, like a Brit, it's equally at home beside a bowl of curry as it is to a plate of fish and chips. As for the title of the beer, *British IPA*, in the late 1800s, British soldiers occupying India were given a ration of six pints of IPA...every day. At this time, these beers were between 10-14% alcohol. Cheers, b'ys.

Eric's Cream Ale

ABV & TYPE: 5% Cream Ale

APPEARANCE: Pours clear and the colour of a brass trumpet, with an orange hue befitting of its coppery taste

AROMA: A gentle aromal. Hints of plum or cut apples maybe

TEXTURE: Creamy, naturally, though crisp as well. It's a fizzy beer, medium-leaning-light in body. A cold-lagering process imparts its smooth mouthfeel

TASTE: More sweet than dry. Essentially a smooth and easy-drinking ale, with some nice hints of whisky, apple, vanilla, and copper. It's great for folks wanting both character and crushability

BEHIND THE BEER: Quidi Vidi has been brewing this one since the turn of the century: Eric's Cream Ale was the Silver Medal Winner at the 2001 World Beer Championships in Chicago. As the brewery says, "Eric's Cream Ale is an excellent choice for those looking for a beer with a little more character while still being extremely approachable." That is the purpose of a cream ale after all: to marry the character of an ale with the refreshment of a lager.

It was originally called Eric's Red because this beer was first named after the famous Viking, Eric The Red, to celebrate the 1000th anniversary of the Viking's landing in L'anse Aux Meadows. A thousand-year-old Viking settlement is a pretty big deal: Eric beat the Brit-funded "discovery" of Newfoundland by 500 years, and unlike the Europeans, Eric and his people let the natives be and fled the island.

It was first brewed with the intention of being a seasonal beer, and featured a Viking themed bottle but the name and packaging was recently changed to avoid any confusion about this beer being a red ale, when it is in fact a cream ale.

What are you looking at?

WHAT ARE YOU LOOKING AT? Eric's Cream Ale also made some waves with an ad campaign that countered the sexist nature of most beer ads. It featured a sprung old man in his underwear. "Our friend Dr. Buehler was a prof at MUN. He was a good friend of the brewery and loved our beer. We decided that every other beer company was doing girls in bikinis, so we'd do the opposite."

Honey Brown

ABV & TYPE: 5% Brown Ale

APPEARANCE: Penny-like colour and clear. Little head, with a little lace

AROMA: The aroma is a whiff of Billy Bee honey on bread, with hints of grain, caramel, malt nuttiness, and maybe some field flowers

TEXTURE: Semi-rich and semi-smooth, with a medium-light body and a crisp mouthfeel that makes it a refreshing beer with a little heartiness too. Medium, prickly carbonation that lasts

TASTE: Taste like it smells: honey-forward. It's a balanced beer, but its gentle hopping makes it lean sweet with any hop bitterness appearing near the end of a sip. Aftertaste is sweet and dry. Hard to put a finger on the hop flavour: it's more bright and floral than it is citrusy or resinous. Starts out coppery before it fills the mouth with smooth and sweet Billy Bee style honey. Its finish leans biscuit caramel with the honey trying to linger for a lasting impression. If you really get in there there's apples and croutons

BEHIND THE BEER: On their brewery tours, Quidi Vidi like to get a little mysterious about this one. "All of our beers use only the essential four ingredients—water, malt, hops, and yeast—except one of them, which we won't name." Surprise, it's likely this beer, and honey is likely the fifth ingredient. Or is that too simple of a conclusion? Take the tour and take it up with their guide, or just relish the mystery in the bottle.

Quidi Vidi Honey Brown is a brown ale, which are brown-coloured matly ales, lightly hopped, and made from brown malts. It's the malts that really punch through here, and Quidi Vidi creates this beer with "a precise combination of chocolate and crystal malts." Chocolate malts taste as you'd expect them too, and crystal malt imparts a caramel flavour, largely because they are roasted at a high temperatures, caramelizing the sugars. They also beef up body, as detectable in a Honey Brown.

Iceberg

ABV & TYPE: 4.5% Lager

APPEARANCE: Notably clear, like transparent straw

AROMA: Faint, leans malt grains and wheat

TEXTURE: Crisp with moderate soda-like carbonation. Smooth, soft, and clean. Soft is the best word here. It's the ultimate easy-drinking beer

TASTE: A malt-forward beer with semi-buttery toasted grains, and hints of hay, minerals, caramel, and something nearly floral. Little in the way of hops, with a sweet backbone and low bitterness. There's a little tang going on too

BEHIND THE BEER: Iceberg Beer visually stands out for two reasons: it's sold in bright cobalt-blue bottles with the mainland long neck. Originally, Iceberg was sold in a clear bottle, but after a clever marketing experiment to make this unique beer look as unique as it tastes, they started selling it in blue bottles.

What makes this beer stand out the most, though, is that it's made from iceberg water, which gives the beer something unusual that beer lovers can't help but be curious about. The folks at Quidi Vidi knew that water quality matters, and iceberg water happens to be the purest water in the world. And iceberg water is also the softest water in the world: pure, soft water makes the best beer, so it's actually a no-brainer.

The brewery employs iceberg harvesters to harvest the chunks of icebergs. It's a dangerous affair. Harvesters tend to wait around until the bergs run aground, and use a big mechanical jaw to bore into the bellies of these glacial beasts and grab ice from deep inside. These chunks are thrown into a hopper and pulverised, and brought to the brewery.

For a light and easy drinking beer, it's gold. And very refreshing. Iceberg took home the bronze medal at the Canadian Brewing Awards in 2014. Story goes, the year they launched Iceberg Beer, an iceberg snaked its way into The Gut in Quidi Vidi and perched itself in the small harbour, as if a wink and a sign they were onto something.

QV Light

ABV & TYPE: 4% Lager

APPEARANCE: A very clear beer, golden hay in colour

AROMA: Sweet malty smells, no hops. It's mainly wheat on the nose, with a little syrup near the end

TEXTURE: Light in body and crisp: a very easy drinking beer. Moderate soda-like carbonation

TASTE: This is a nice and refreshing light lager. It's entirely malt-forward, with little in the way of hops beyond its counterbalancing weedy bite. Its main tastes are wheat, malt biscuit, some bread and syrup, and that distinctive Quidi Vidi copper tang. There's also just a touch of sour key candy in the finish to give it a nice acidic snap

BEHIND THE BEER: Roughly 65% of beer consumed in Newfoundland is light beer. In other provinces, that number is more like 25-30%. Maybe Newfoundlanders like it light because we drink it in bulk: NL is the second biggest consumer of beer in the country.

With stats like that in their province of operation, it's no wonder Quidi Vidi made a light beer to cater to that demand. And they really nailed it, it's a great light lager for a province of light-lager lovers. It was a smart move to launch QV Light in their second year of operation. The beer is credited with boosting sales by more than 50%.

Quidi Vidi introduced this light beer as "Northern Light," with a beer label drawn by local artist Danielle Loranger, depicting the St. John's harbour. Northern Light was renamed to QV Light because some mainland brewery in Ontario was making a brand called Northern Light.

The brewery itself says Quidi Vidi Light is the ultimate easy drinking beer, and in that regard, it's exactly what it aims to be: an easy-drinking beer that's a real step up from a Coors or Canadian Light. It's clean, crisp, and easy to drink a pile of at a dayboil, or after a big meal at your pal's birthday BBQ.

 It's also really good with a shot of tequila, and a bunch of lime juice and salt poured into it.

Quidi Vidi Premium

ABV & TYPE: 5% Lager

APPEARANCE: Clear and golden, with a short, loose head. No lace

AROMA: Biscuity/grainy malts, maybe a little apple, minerals, and tomato-on-a-vine

TEXTURE: Medium in body, with a moderate carbonation. A little creamy

TASTE: Moderately sweet, mildly bitter, with a quick smack of sour near the end. Medium sweetness from the malts is more pronounced than its grassy hop profile, but it's generously hopped for a lager. Predominant flavour would be its bready malt character, with some green apple, corn-on-the-cob, and a coppery mineral taste. As far as this book is concerned, it's one of Quidi Vidi's top 3 in the taste department

BEHIND THE BEER: For a lager it's really quite expressive, hopped, and flavourful, and has that nice crisp lager quality in conjunction with its ale-like flavour. It's near and dear to the hearts of many fans of this brewery, so it's a surprise this one is a rarity on taps in town and around the island (you'll find Iceberg, British IPA, and 1892 almost anywhere).

"It's our only 5% lager and the only beer we don't put in kegs. That reason is top secret however!" Not to spread any unfounded gossip, but unconfirmed rumours and urban myths declare Premium is actually equal parts 1892 and Honey Brown mixed together in a giant vat! That urban myth seems unlikely given they're ales, and this is a lager.

Whatever its secrets are, Quidi Vidi Premium took home a silver medal at the 2014 Canadian Brewing Awards in the category of North American Style Lager.

A FITTING SETTING FOR THEIR BREWERY
Scudrunner's Brewery and Taproom is an open
concept, with an industrial hangar motif.

SCUDRUNNER BREWING

2018, GANDER

It's no surprise, given Gander's history of aviation, that two pilots gave flight to the town's only brewery. David Jarrett and Sam Newman worked together often, as First Officer and Captain on the same aircraft, and craft beer was their go-to small talk. Until it became their joint business venture

"Sam and I met while working for Air Canada based out of Gander," says David Jarrett. "I had just returned from living in the U.K., and was missing both the variety of beer in England, and the way that the British relish and celebrate beer culture."

Sam had been brewing beer at home for many years, and introduced David to the Newfoundland and Labrador Craft and Artisanal Beer Club. "We started brewing together at home on our days off, and haven't stopped yet."

David says that integration of local culture and experimentation with local ingredients is common in Europe, and Scudrunner wanted to create a home for that in Central Newfoundland. Their name, Scudrunner Brewing, is taken from the plane industry. Scud running is the art of navigating an aircraft around many small clouds (scuds) to get to the airport, or lake of choice for landing. "We wanted a name that reflects the importance of aviation to us, and to Central Newfoundland, and the fact that aviation was what brought Sam and I together," David says.

"To me, the name reflects a sense of ingenuity that Newfoundlanders have. Newfoundlanders take pride in creating their own solutions, and using their hands to create what they need, rather than rely on others to do it for them." Similarly, he adds, Scudrunner is about making a quality product with their own hands, in a building they designed and created on their own.

Speaking of their space, it's located at 131 Roe Avenue. It is open concept, with an industrial hangar motif. Patrons can observe the brewery operation while sampling beers in their taproom.

SCUDRUNNER TOOK FLIGHT IN MARCH OF 2018 It was launched by two pilots who were often First Officer and Captain on the same aircraft. Craft beer was their go-to small talk. Until it became their joint business venture. Pictured are co-founders David Jarrett and Sam Newman.

As for food, they may work towards having a small menu, but welcome people to take their own food in from neighbouring restaurants or stores. They're in the business of beer, they say, and don't want to get in the way of the town's existing dining options. On their travels to other breweries in other countries, what they loved as much as the beer was seeing how microbreweries can be real community hubs to bring people together, particularly as hosts of local events or as players in community collaborations.

"We were lucky to work with Ian Hallett, a graphic designer in Toronto (and my wife's step-father!) to create an aviation and Newfoundland inspired taproom. We used local, recycled, and sustainable products in its creation whenever possible. We were also lucky to work with a Canadian company, who created us a state of the art brew house. It is a ten hectolitre system which uses a novel digital control system. This allows us to perfect, and perfectly repeat, our recipes."

Head Brewer Sam Newman got into brewing as far back as childhood, intrigued by his father's dedication to homebrewing. But a European honeymoon with stops in beer havens like the Netherlands and Germany solidified his status as a true brewer. While in Germany, he adopted their "Reinheitsgebot" philosophy and brought it to the table as an integral part of the Scudrunner Brewing operation.

Scudrunner existed as a quality homebrewing operation for a while before they opened a legit microbrewery. They served enough homebrew beer at tastings, catered events, and fine-dining occasions in Gander to have built a reputation and demand prior to building an official brewery.

The beer's reception among attendees of these events inspired them to cash in on their craft. "The only question was how do we go from a 5-gallon brewday to a 5-barrel brewday," Sam jokes. Their slow take-off meant they'd been building Scudrunner's beer list—tinkering with tastes and recipes—for a long time before the brewery opened.

Now that they're open, they vow to settle for nothing but "top quality, premium craft beer. After all," they add, "who enjoys a cold one more than a hard-working Newfoundlander?"

Scudrunner launched offering 4 core beers: Canadian Pale Ale, Special IPA, a Helles, and a Dunkel. "Primarily, we make beer that we love to drink. Seasonal flavours celebrating local communities are in the works." This book was published too soon for details on their Helles and Dunkel, alas, here are some details on their other two.

Canadian Pale Ale

ABV & TYPE: 5.5% Pale Ale

APPEARANCE: Bright, golden straw. Clean, white head

AROMA: Fresh, light, and nutty. Inviting

TEXTURE: Light body. Strong carbonation

TASTE: Tangy, clean, and dry. Malt forward. Sharp earthy tones of pine, honey, and grasses. Prepares and entices the palate for a meal

BEHIND THE BEER: A flavour spectrum including pine, it doesn't get any more Canadian than that. Scudrunner calls this one a truly Canadian beer, as it was designed to showcase all the qualities of beer Canadians have collectively come to love.

Using fresh, Canadian-grown ingredients, they put the Canadian in "American Pale Ale" with this recipe, which utilizes a unique, clean-fermenting Canadian yeast that they say "melds complex, earthy flavours into a harmonious, pleasing pan-palate feel."

"This beer simplifies and emphasizes the flavours we all love about Canadian beer."

Lovebirds IPA

ABV & TYPE: 6% IPA

APPEARANCE: Brilliant red, clear. Thick, creamy head

AROMA: Deep, strong sustained layers of hops and malt

TEXTURE: Full body. Moderate to high carbonation

TASTE: Dry and dense. Combines the strong and complex hoppy flavour of the American style New England IPA with the slightly more subtle earthy maltiness of a traditional red ale. The parallel flavours hit the front of the palate together, and finish together, leaving you wanting more

BEHIND THE BEER: Scudrunner's Special IPA was inspired by the international success of the popular broadway musical Come From Away, which dramatized the events of 9/11 as they took place in Gander.

Specifically, it was inspired by the musical love story. "English and American ingredients and styles are combined in a unique way, similar to the meeting of a British man and American woman in the play," they say. "The strong hops, and more subtle malt come together in a flavour more complete and interesting than they are apart."

This "special IPA" really is something special, as it does something unexpected in merging the hop qualities of a New England Style IPA with the earthy maltiness of a red ale. Can't decide what you want a pint of, why not grab a glass of something boasting 2-styles-in-1?

"This is a beer you will want with you to complement a piece of red meat and plate of veg," they suggest.

SPLIT ROCK
SPLIT ROCK
BREWING CO.
Twillingate, Newfoundland

SPLIT ROCK BREWING CO.

2017, TWILLINGATE

The origin of Split Rock Brewing Co. was a combination of chance, and the limited degrees of separation between family and friends in a rural town like Twillingate.

Everyone kinda knows everyone in Twillingate, and that made it so much easier for happenstance and serendipity to help a new brewery open its doors to the people (and visitors) of the province. Music helped too. Perhaps more than any other province, music really brings people together in Newfoundland, and it's ultimately what brought the forces behind Split Rock together.

Robin Vatcher played in a band called Nightshift, with Matt Vincent's father many years ago, and Matt would "bum around with them and help set up their gear," so they knew each other. Cue to many years later, and Vatcher, a businessman by trade, saw an old eyesore of a building on Main Street, and bought it to "do something with." It was Matt's passion for beer that gave Vatcher that "something to do with the building" he was looking for. But only because of a coincidence.

Robin's son, Tim Vatcher, had a baby on the way, and it just so happened that his wife, Ann-Marie, was in pre-natal classes with Matt Vincent's wife (Matt's wife, Allison, is as much a brewer and beer lover as Matt is). She and Tim Vatcher's wife got to talking about what a great idea a brewery would be for Twillingate...and how Tim's father had just bought a building that would be perfect for it.

So Split Rock Brewing Co. was born as easily as that, though naming it wasn't so easy. "A few names were tossed around, but nothing really felt right. Matt pitched the idea of Split Rock because Twillingate is made up of two islands, and the brewery location is right where the Town is 'split in two.' It had a good ring to it, and a friend of ours designed a logo that we loved."

SPLIT ROCK WAS ROCKING AWARD WINNING STATUS FROM THE START These guys opened in the same season as the 2017 Atlantic Canadian Beer Awards. They came home from their first competition with a medal for "Alli's Big Brown Ale."

Prior to opening the brewery, Matt and Allison had been in Halifax for 12 years. During the latter end of that stint of living away, Halifax's craft-beer scene was booming, and it got them excited about brewing.

"We started making wines in our apartment in Dartmouth," they said. "We had a growing interest in trying different varieties and comparing one against another. Meanwhile, the craft-beer scene was growing in Halifax-Dartmouth and we loved it. Matt decided to pick up a beer kit at the wine store (not your regular powered kit), and it was pretty good. We heard about people brewing from extract and 'all-grain' and we were immediately intrigued. When we purchased our first home in 2010, we finally had the space to take our homebrewing to the next level."

Once Matt and Allison began homebrewing all-grain style, the dream of opening a microbrewery followed. They had a "microbrewery fund" piggy bank going for years before Split Rock's founders (The Vincent spouses and the Vatcher father and son) ever came together.

Split Rock Brewing Co. strives for approachable beers largely inspired by classic English styles. Upon opening, they said, "we'll be brewing our favourites of course—English ales, an IPA for the hop heads and a Belgian Witbier. We're hoping to get creative with some seasonal brews once we really get up and running."

By offering 7 core beers out of the gates, Matt promises they make something for everyone's palate and preferences. Seven beers sounds like a lot to have started with, but Matt brews on a 500-litre system from Colorado Brewing Systems that is capable of a full brewday in only four hours.

Their taproom has 8 taps, all of which are Split Rock's core beers and seasonal offerings. Their brewery is adjoined to their lively pub: the Stage Head Pub.

Six of their seven core beers are listed below. Their 7th beer will always be an IPA of some kind, but ever changing. "Most times it will be an American style showcasing citrusy American hops," but in keeping with their love of English ales, Matt says, "We may mix it up from time to time with an English variation as well."

Alli's Big Brown Ale

ABV & TYPE: 5.6% Brown Ale

APPEARANCE: Brown with a tan head

AROMA: Toast, nuts, and chocolate

TEXTURE: Medium body, low-medium carbonation

TASTE: Malt-forward sweetness with a complementary grain/hop bitterness.

Roasted malts shine in this beer with a toasty, nutty flavour

BEHIND THE BEER: This recipe was born when Brewmaster Matt challenged his wife Alli to design her own beer from the ground up. She wanted to brew a beer that had all of her favourite things: a full-bodied brown ale that was balanced, nutty, chocolatey, and malty.

Alli describes the resulting beer as "tea and PB toast." They all say it was one of their favourite brew days while gearing up to launch their brewery, and it yielded this impressive, welcome addition to the beers of Newfoundland, as there certainly aren't many brown ales going around.

	ON TAP	ABV	Growl Fill
1	Combines Ale	5.3%	✓
2	Bluff Head Bitter	4.6%	✓
3	Gateway IPA	6.7%	✓
4	Red Sky Red Rye	4.9%	✓
5	Alli's Big Brown Ale	5.6%	✓
6	Black Island Stout	6.1%	✓
7			
8			

Combines Ale

ABV & TYPE: 5.3% Cream Ale

APPEARANCE: Light straw colour, white head

AROMA: Minimal; slightly fruity

TEXTURE: Light body, effervescent

TASTE: Dry, well attenuated, easy-drinking, and refreshing

BEHIND THE BEER: Built to be a thirst quencher, say, after a game of hockey, this ale is named after a local hockey team. "Due to this being a 100% malt/non-adjunct beer," they say, "it has more flavour than your average cream ale."

Bluff Head Bitter

ABV & TYPE: 5% Bitter

APPEARANCE: Amber colour, off-white head

AROMA: Moderate English hop character, fruity and biscuity

TEXTURE: Light body, effervescent

TASTE: Malty with balanced hop bitterness

BEHIND THE BEER: Alli got to brew her favourite beer in Split Rock's "Alli's Big Brown Ale," and Matt got to do the same here, with their English Bitter (his favourite style). Bitters are relatives of pale ales, but with less alcohol and carbonation, and less tongue-snapping bitterness.

"It's easy-drinking, but full of flavour," he says, "and the English yeast characteristics really come through in this beer."

Red Sky Red Rye

ABV & TYPE: 5% Red / Rye Ale

APPEARANCE: Red with a tan-coloured head

AROMA: Rye spices, pleasant maltyness, with notes of caramel and toffee

TEXTURE: Medium body with a creamy, slick mouthfeel

TASTE: A sweet and malty backbone that blends nicely with the spiciness of the rye

BEHIND THE BEER: "As the saying goes, red sky at night is a sailor's delight, and this beer is definitely a delight for Red Ale lovers," Matt says.

"We created this recipe because we wanted to do something a little different with our red ale, and we had a bunch of malted rye on our shelf. This recipe doesn't fit into a specific category and we love its unique character." This distinct ale is definitely a welcome addition to Newfoundland's beer offerings for lovers of red or rye ales, and particularly for lovers of both those styles.

Black Island Stout

ABV & TYPE: 6.1% Stout

APPEARANCE: Black colour, brown head

AROMA: Roasted malt, chocolate

TEXTURE: Medium body, low-medium carbonation

TASTE: Earthy, roasted coffee/chocolate flavour

BEHIND THE BEER: For all the new breweries on the island, there's not a lot of offerings in the way of stouts beyond YellowBelly's St. John's Stout. Split Rock's opening in 2017 plugged a lot of holes in Newfoundland's beer scene.

"We spent a lot of time working on our stout. It started as an oatmeal stout, but we switched up the oats for some flaked barley."

Twitty Witty

ABV & TYPE: 4.8% Belgian Witbier

APPEARANCE: Light straw colour, cloudy, white head

AROMA: Orange fruitiness, coriander spice

TEXTURE: Light-medium body, highly carbonated

TASTE: Light and refreshing, mildly tart, zesty orange and spicy yeast-derived flavours

BEHIND THE BEER: It's hard to top a Witbier, especially under a full summer sun. They are made following a Belgian tradition of spicing the beer with fruits and herbs, normally coriander and orange peel, and using a lot of wheat as the grain as opposed to 100% barley. It's the suspended, unfiltered yeast and wheat proteins that cause them to look hazy.

"This is our favourite summer beer," Split Rock says, "Coriander and Orange peel, along with a Belgian yeast strain, produces an interesting and refreshing beer."

STORM BREWING

1995, MOUNT PEARL

In 1995, Storm Brewing, named to reflect the harsh marine environment of New-foundland, was the province's first independent craft brewery to emerge since Atlantic Brewery/Bison Brewing shuttered in the seventies. When Storm started brewing, it had been over 22 years since Newfoundland had a local microbrewery.

Storm Brewing started out as Freshwater Brewing, in Carbonear, but its co-founders, Nick Murray and Dave Rodgers, parted ways in 1997. Nick and Beth Murray acquired it, renamed it to Storm, moved the brewery into Mt. Pearl, and approached Michael McBride and his wife Kristi to become partners in the brewery.

Michael and Kristi run the show now, using equipment purchased from the defunct Santa Rosa Brewing Co. in California. Michael has been Atlantic Canada's representative on the National Brewers' Association Board.

Storm operates out of a non-public space in Mt. Pearl, so there's no taproom, but you can find them on tap at select pubs in St. John's, like The Ship and The Duke of Duckworth. Like many beer enthusiasts, they prefer ales to lagers, and in fact they've only ever made ales.

Storm currently brew 2 core beers—Island Gold and Newfoundland Irish Red—plus a regular winter seasonal, Coffee Porter, and regular summer seasonal, Raspberry Wheat, though it is not uncommon to spot some of these in shoulder seasons on shelves at the NLC.

Storm has been experimental in its history, and collaborative. Their wildest venture might have been their now-retired hemp ale. Shortly after it was approved for production, Storm Hemp Ale was shut down over a variety of red flags. The way McBride tells the story is that "Under the Presidency of George W. Bush, it became increasingly difficult to source sterilized hemp seeds." It's a shame, it was a good beer with a nice nutty flavour. But McBride has implied that a return of their Hemp Ale may be in the works.

FREE NFLD A lot of people wonder what happened to Storm's Free NFLD Beer, which was sold in stubby bottles. Nothing, really. It was their Irish Red sold with this label is all.

They also use their facilities to brew for others. For example, "The Duke's Own" at the Duke of Duckworth is a recipe brewed by Storm. When the Duke expanded its kitchen, they had to gut their brewing operation, and could no longer brew The Duke's Own onsite anymore, so Storm make it for them now. It is, however, Storm's recipe now, not The Duke's.

One thing that stands out about their beer is the sheer look of the bottles. They sell singles in bomber bottles, and their half cases come in standard longer-necked mainland beer bottles, not the short-necked "BOB 21" bottles all other local beers are sold in. Originally they used stubby bottles, and many will remember the years in the mid-2000s when they sold their Irish Red in stubbies with a popular "Free NFLD" label. The time came when they could no longer source them in North America, so they switched to the Industry Standard Bottle.

Originally, Storm used Auntie Crae's coffee in their recipe, but Auntie Crae's have closed their storefront. Now they use another local operation: Jumping Bean. The pairing of humanity's favourite beverages—coffee and beer—is as good as it sounds, and begs the question of why coffee porters aren't more common.

Chef Stephen featured Storm's Coffee Porter as the beverage pairing for his entry into the Gold Metal Plates in 2010. Coffee Porters like this one pair well with Indian dishes, or Szechuan-based ones, as well as berry cheesecakes, or cheeses like Stilton, feta, and Roquefort.

Coffee Porter

ABV & TYPE: 5% Porter

APPEARANCE: Dark brown, with medium opacity. Looks like a glass of Coke in the glass. Not much head, plenty of lace

AROMA: Coffee, naturally, and dark chocolate. There's some molasses and liquorice in there too

TEXTURE: It's mild, smooth, and medium-bodied. Low carbonation as you'd expect. A nice and dry-ish finish makes you want another sip

TASTE: It's roasty, and much like its smell in taste: coffee, dark chocolate, bread, and molasses. Slightly herbal hop notes, some sour notes, some leathery ones

BEHIND THE BEER: Storm's Coffee Porter is normally only available from October to April. It is brewed using imported black malt, and locally purchased coffee beans, which complement each other strikingly well. This brew was inspired from a trip its brewmaster took to coffee country, Columbia, in 2000.

Island Gold

ABV & TYPE: 5% Ale

APPEARANCE: Light copper in colour and fairly opaque; a little head and lasting lace

AROMA: Earthy and floral, with notes of one-cent candy. Some minerals

TEXTURE: A light beer approaching medium in body. Its light carbonation and smoothness imparts an almost stout-like mouthfeel. There's a semi-dry finish

TASTE: Slightly hoppy (grassy) with a salted-cracker and toffee malt profile. Hints of white wine. The hoppiness is pronounced but dissolves in a blanket of semi-sweetness. There's an earthy orange flavour in there, with some metals, minerals and hints of fruity esters as a finish

BEHIND THE BEER: Storm's Island Gold Ale was brewed to "combine the best elements of an ale with a refreshing character." The end result is indeed a refreshing beer, hard to pin a specific taste to. If you're in for long-haul drinking some night, and prefer ale over a lager, bring this one to the party. It's something anyone from a Coors drinker to a craft drinker will be happy to be handed late in the evening.

This crowd pleaser took third place during "Show One" of the first ever St. John's Brewfest in 2016.

Irish Red

ABV & TYPE: 5.5% Red Ale

APPEARANCE: The colour and clarity of Coca-Cola with a deep red hue, and a bit of short-lived head

AROMA: A nice smoky scent, beside a sweet-malty smell bordering on candy-ish. Notes of toffee, coffee, caramel, honey, and spices

TEXTURE: A light-to-medium bodied beer with prickly carbonation results in a soda-like mouthfeel. There's a dry finish with little after taste

TASTE: A toasted malt quality, with a light-hop character. Its bitterness is balanced by a real rainbow of nice malt flavours: caramel, coffee, toffee, brown sugar, butterscotch, a little buttered toast. Overall, a treat for lovers of malty brews. There are woody spices or toasted nuts at the end too

BEHIND THE BEER: Storm's Irish Red is a rebel of a red, and that's what they were going for. Storm considers this their own unique twist on the Irish Red style.

STORM ON THE BIG SCREEN Rob Wells, aka "Ricky" from Trailer Park Boys, drinks Storm beers in the movie Beat Down.

It was initially named Kyle, after the famous shipwreck of the *SS Kyle*, whose weather-rusted carcass is still sticking out of the water in Harbour Grace. Despite her rugged nickname of "The Bulldog of the North," the boat ran aground on the shore of Riverhead, Harbour Grace, in the winter of 1967, after decades of transporting people and supplies from Carbonear to Labrador. The Kyle also used to transport foot soldiers from Newfoundland to Canada during World War II.

Raspberry Wheat

ABV & TYPE: 5% Wheat Ale.

APPEARANCE: A clear, amber-orange colour with little head or lace.

AROMA: The raspberry is there, along with a broader wildberry smell, with a little caramel, spiced tea, hay, and herbaceous hop.

TEXTURE: An appropriately light, crisp, and refreshing ale, with prickly carbonation. Finishes sweet with a mildly tangy aftertaste.

TASTE: Its slightly sweet raspberry flavour is prominent, balanced with a tang. The slight hop bitterness marries well with the raspberry-tart sweetness. There's also some herby hops, and more wheat on the tongue than in the nose

BEHIND THE BEER: Brewed only in the summer, this beer is brewed using water, wheat, barley malts, hops, yeast, and a touch of pure raspberry extract to impart its refreshing raspberry aroma. Storm market its "clean, zesty flavour." They were inspired to make their summer seasonal a raspberry wheat because of one specific beer: Kawartha Lakes Brewing's Raspberry Wheat.

This isn't a sickly or syrupy raspberry wheat ale, it's a proper one, and it took home second place for Best Brew at Show Two during the first ever St. John's Brewfest in 2016.

A WILD VENTURE Storm Hemp Ale, c. mid-2000s. [Photo: Colin Power]

YELLOWBELLY BREWERY

2008, ST. JOHN'S

YellowBelly Brewery has the kind of brewmaster they can brag about. Liam McKenna's beer is so good that when he was making beer in Dublin, Guinness bullied Irish pub owners into not stocking his stout. You know you've made the right career choice when the world's biggest brand of beer thinks you're a serious threat.

Liam alone makes all of YellowBelly's beer, and if you sit and talk with this man about beer, what it is, and what it should be, you're reminded of why they call his job a brewMASTER. He's been dubbed "the great polemicist of the craft brewing movement" by *The Irish Times*. A polemicist is a person with very strong opinions—no doubt they were referring to his strict ethos on, and passion for what good beer is.

"Freshness is tremendously important," he's told *The Overcast*. "To brewers, beer is a kind of liquid bread. I would not buy bread from Germany or Mexico, so why would I buy beer from there? It doesn't travel well." A commitment to quality and craft steered his decision to work in local craft brewpubs over big international breweries.

"Small brewing has offered me the kind of control and influence over the process and the products that would be totally unavailable to me in an industrial scene."

After decades of working in microbreweries, McKenna's awards include medals at the World Beer Championships, the Stockholm Beer Festival, and the Brewing Industry International Awards. Acclaimed beverage writer Billy Munnelly has called him "Canada's Best Brewmaster."

McKenna is a microbiologist by academic background. "I struggled with schooling until beer and brewing seemed to pull it into a focus. I found brewing to be a very good mixture of art and science. The microbrewing scene was just getting started, and after a few work terms at various breweries, I decided to pursue the small brewery route."

PUTTING THE MASTER IN BREWMASTER Legend has it, Liam McKenna makes stouts so good, Guiness once bullied pub owners not to stock his for fear of competition. Why not line up a Guiness beside a YellowBelly St. John's Stout some night, just for fun.

Microbrewing also lets him avoid additives. "Time, design, appropriate processes, and equipment can remove the need to use any or all additives. The per capita consumption of beer in Canada is about 85 litres/year. That can be pure and natural if you want. People like me will continue to ensure that."

Working in a microbrewery also lets McKenna bang out one-off small-batch or seasonal beers all year long. And they're always too good to miss. You can buy them as pints, or in bomber bottles to go atYellowBelly, or occasionally score them at an NLC outlet.

"From conception to actualization, we can introduce a new product in as little as three weeks. That process in large breweries can take years." He's made some legendary small-batch beers, one of which was their "Hard Tack Ale" that used day-old bread from Rocket Bakery down the road: waste not want not! People still talk about his turnip pale ale that, yes, used turnip in its recipe. YellowBelly's annual Mummer's Brew is also something to anticipate every Christmas. But Liam's personal favourite, and the people's pick, is the YB signature beer: YellowBelly Pale Ale.

YellowBelly Brewery is also a city favourite for pubfare, being a true brewpub. Best known for their wood-fired pizzas, they've been featured on The Food Network's popular program, "You Gotta Eat Here." It has multiple floors and a small patio. Its building was originally constructed in 1725, making it one of the oldest structures in North America. Luckily, the building was re-constructed in 1846, with brick, because that brick walling is what made this building the place where the "Great Fire of 1892" was finally extinguished; the building resisted "The Great Fire" that burned the rest of the town down to the ground. You can see some scorching of the 1892 fire in the wooden beams downstairs in The Underbelly—YellowBelly's speakeasy style bar in the basement.

As for the name, YellowBelly, it harkens back to the Irish immigrants who came to Newfoundland between 1750 and 1830. The "Yellowbellies" were an Irish faction hailing from Wexford who famously tied strips of yellow cloth around their mid-sections in a hurling match against the Cornish champions. Following their victory, King George III remarked, "Well done the Yellowbellies!" and it stuck.

Irishmen from County Wexford living in St. John's back in the day identified themselves by wearing yellow sashes around their bellies. They'd hang out at the corner of Beck's Cove and Water Street, and this corner—where YellowBelly Brewery now stands—became known as YellowBelly Corner.

Fighting Irish Red

ABV & TYPE: 5.5% Red Ale

APPEARANCE: So deeply red it's garnet and opaque. Its tan head is quite adhesive as lace and provides a nice colour contrast

AROMA: Big malty notes on the nose, with coffee, toffee, molasses, brown sugar, chocolate, and caramel at the fore. It's an impossible bouquet of delicious malt scents that all punch through individually. It's also a little nutty, with hints of nostalgic campsmoke. This beer is intensely, or rather, impressively aromatic. There's no sign of that yeasty, bland, undescript "beer smell"

TEXTURE: Thick in body, mouthfeel, and complexity; easy on carbonation

TASTE: With its notes of strawberry jam on homemade toast, and a hefty portion of cappuccino and molasses on the side, you could almost call this one a meal, if not the best brunch pint in town. It's marked by a multitude of roasty malt flavours, ending with a nice, very long finish where its grassy bitter notes come out to say hi. The recipe's roasted barley adds all those complex and varied malt tastes, including the hint of leather and Toffifees. There's something nutty and woody afoot here too. A nice dry finish punches through in the aftertaste

BEHIND THE BEER: If you're familair with popular pints on taps worldwide, Liam McKenna has described this beer as YellowBelly's answer to Ricard's Red. His exact words were,"Think Rickard's Red on crack."

Like all of Yellowbelly's ales, it pays tribute to UK beer traditions, and this is a straight-up traditional Irish Red that will impress fans of the style. Their Fighting Irish Red is no stranger to media attention, having landed on lists like Huffington Post's "20 Great Canadian Beers," where it sat besides popular Canadian faves like St-Ambroise Oatmeal Stout and Unibroue's Fin du Monde. Yellowbelly themselves describe it as their most complex beer, hence its suggested pairing with spicy foods and game meats.

Fighting Irish Red is a malt lovers' paradise, with an impossible bouquet of malt tastes and smells. The label has an old Irishmen with his dukes up, and appropriately so: this traditional red ale could throw down with the best of what's offered by any Canadian brewers brewing Irish Red Ales.

St. John's Stout

ABV & TYPE: 4.8% Stout

APPEARANCE: Black like oil is, with a creamy head.

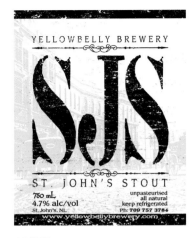

AROMA: Dark chocolate, coffee, fresh tobacco, vanilla, and roasted nuts.

TEXTURE: Smooth and creamy. Very low carbonation (even for a stout; this one feels like a cask ale in the mouth), so it goes down the hatch quite danger-easily for a stout. There's silkiness in the mouthfeel that comes from the liberal use of malted oats.

TASTE: Roasty flavours from the malt, and interestingly,on account of much hopping in the kettle, there's additional bitterness from the roasted barley. Overall, it's a mouthful of liquorice, coffee, dark chocolate, and burnt toast from the malt spectrum, with some cedar and lemon on the hop spectrum, balanced well. If you really dive in, there's some earthy nuts

BEHIND THE BEER: This beer had the distinction of being the only stout brewed on the island between 2008 and the 2017 surge of new breweries, and maybe because people were intimidated to put something up against it.

You have no doubt heard of and drank a

Guinness—it is sold internationally and stands as the most popular, best branded stout in the world. So it says a lot about Liam McKenna, brewer of the St. John's Stout, that Guinness used to coerce or pay Irish pub owners money not to stock Liam's beers in their bars when Liam was making beer in the UK.

So, is the St. John's Stout actually better than Guinness? The forces behind this book can say with honesty they go head to head. But then all of our tastes differ, and better is a relative term. (*But yes, it's better.*)

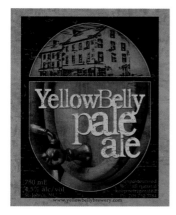

YellowBelly Pale Ale

ABV & TYPE: 4.5% Pale Ale

APPEARANCE: There's nothing "pale" about it; for a pale ale, this beer has a striking dark-amber bronze colour, with beautiful lustre and clarity. Plenty of foam head and so much lace its painting the pint glass here. Unmistakably a craft beer made with care

AROMA: This beer is dry hopped, and you can tell on that first whiff: it's full of piney-citrusy hop scents, that do not overwhelm the beer's bready and caramelly malt notes

TEXTURE: Full-bodied with a medium carbonation and dry finish that lingers. To quote its brewer, "low in alcohol but not in character." It's thick and more creamy than slick

TASTE: For a pale ale, it's lightly hopped enough to be easy drinking—but it does pack a wallop of expressive hop tastes. Most notably, there's fabulous spruce and grapefruit from the hops, balanced by toast and caramel from the malt, and some apiary-grade honey at the finish. There's an interesting fruit note in here too from its fermentation: pineapple? Marmalade? Your sip will start with the sweet malts and end with the aforementioned hops of the citrus-resinous variety

BEHIND THE BEER: This beer was crowned "Best Craft Beer in Town" by readers of *The Overcast* in our 2015 Best of St. John's survey. To quote Lauren Power's article about YB Pale Ale's win in that category, "It's familiar, but not too familiar. It's agreeable enough to be accessible to your average bar patron, but it's got enough craft in it to make beer aficionados tip their glasses in appreciation." It also happens to be its brewmaster's favourite YellowBelly beer, as well as, as he's said, "Our favourite among beer geeks."

In other words, it's a real crowd pleaser, and a pleaser of all crowds, from the avid craft-ale fanatic to the budding microbrew enthusiast, because it packs tons of flavour and mouthfeel, but is gentler in the mouth than its bolder cousins in the craft pale ale world, who are increasingly looking to shock the mouths of those who've already tried it all.

"In a marketplace increasingly encroached upon by major American manufacturers, eating up shelf space by mimicking (or buying out) true craft breweries, YellowBelly Pale Ale is an excellent symbol for success," writes Lauren Power. "It reminds us that local things, done well, by people that care, can become the gold standard."

This beer pairs well with high-calorie pubfoods like burgers, Fish'n'chips, or pizza, which is great, considering it's their lowest calorie-count beer.

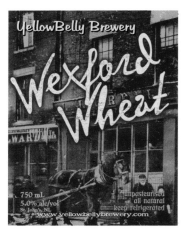

Wexford Wheat

ABV & TYPE: 5% Wheat Ale

APPEARANCE: A cloudy straw yellow bordering on orange in hue. Its notably hazy appearance comes from the protein content in the wheat.

AROMA: Wheat and straw, with a whiff of Del Monte tropical fruit cup (papaya?). Some biscuit malt and bread too.

TEXTURE: Its fairly high carbonation, light body, and apple-tartness make this one a crisp, refreshing, easy drinking beer.

TASTE: To quote its brewer, this one is "sparkling and fresh, lightly hopped, with a clean finish." Liam adds a significant portion of malted wheat in the mash, which gives this brew its distinct green apple and plum skin note in the middle of the palate. It's quite a well-balanced American wheat ale, with a short finish and moreish appeal. Its tropical mango-papaya aroma comes across faintly in the taste too.

BEHIND THE BEER: This American wheat ale is "Yellowbelly's answer to Coors Light" for those who like a pleasantly easy-drinking air beer, that, in this case, tastes great.

When Liam McKenna arrived in Newfoundland to work in YellowBelly as its brewmaster, Coors Light was—and still is—the island's best-selling beer. He knew better than to ignore that, and wanted to give patrons a sort of cross-over beer that could gently introduce Coors-types to craft beer. They could have a pint, join the craft beer club, order another, or try something a little more adventurous. Their call, but, they'd have the option. Which makes sense given the only beers on tap at Yellowbelly brewpub are Yellowbelly's own.

If you happen to order one in YellowBelly's pub, it pairs well with salads, pizzas, and seafood; crab and lobster in particular.

WESTERN NEWFOUNDLAND BREWING CO.

2016, PASADENA

Western Newfoundland Brewing self-describes not as a microbrewery, but even smaller: a nanobrewery. It's located in Pasadena, making them the first company to give craft beer a go on the western half of the island in nearly 50 years.

The brewery is the brain child of Jennifer Galliott and a father and son duo in Jim and Norman MacDonald. Their ties to Gros Morne, the national park that brought them all together, are varied. Jennifer is a fifth generation local from Woody Point, "always looking for yet another excuse to stay in the beautiful area," Jim arrived in Gros Morne on a week-long camping trip five years ago and never left, and Norm "hails from the pollen-laden forests of Eastern Ontario, and likes being able to breathe during allergy season."

Jim met Galliott in 2011, on that camping trip he's still never returned from, because she runs Galliott Studios in Woody Point: a stunning little cafe, pub, and craft shop, whose "patio seating" is actually a wharf in the heart of beautiful Bonne Bay.

Norm had the idea of starting a microbrewery in his head since the mid-1980s, but never knew where he wanted to open it until his trip to the West Coast of Newfoundland. Galliott has always believed a town needs attractive food and drink culture to boost tourism appeal and economic opportunity, and the brewery's wheels started turning the day Norm asked if he could try a local brew on tap at Galliott Studios. She said yes so long as "we worked together towards a common vision."

The result was not a hurried effort. While their commercial production started in the fall of 2016, it was two years of painstaking work to get the vats a-brewing, in part because they took their time in resolving how they could make the product they wanted to make.

"The beer needed to be full-bodied, full-flavoured; The beer could never sacrifice

THE ELUSIVE MERSASQUATCH
For their company logo, Western Newfoundland Brewing Company adopted the little known Newfoundland Mersasquatch. A half merman, half-sasquatch species said to exist only in Northern Gros Morne.

quality for the sake of expedient production or cost-saving measures." They sound happy with the result. "We exceeded our expectations in accomplishing these goals. We pay close attention to the characteristics of each lot of grain, hops, and yeast that we purchase. We know exactly the mineral content of our water and how it needs to be conditioned depending on style."

Water is a vital component of beer, and they're right to stress the quality of theirs. "We brew our beer traditionally in small batches with clean, clear, crisp Western Newfoundland water." Norm's professional background is as a chemical engineer. "His experience has been exceptionally advantageous to refining the quality of our product," says Jim. "He understands how different sugar chains, proteins, and acids will contribute beneficially or deleteriously to the quality of the beer."

Before opening their own doors, they went knocking on the doors of other brewers in Atlantic Canada. "We have watched the growth of craft beer in Nova Scotia, New Brunswick, and Prince Edward Island and were lucky enough to take the opportunity to tour a number of these facilities and extensively pick the brains of their operators. Each one of them is doing something special."

They say their "style and strategy" has been especially influenced by Beau's, just outside of Ottawa. "They began with a defunct textile factory, a lot of willpower, and some eye-catching ceramic bottles. Ten years later they're one of the largest independent brewers in the country and all of their products are incredibly well-balanced and refined."

They also admire Toronto's Steamwhistle, "simply for their dedication to doing a fantastic job on just one style of beer. Steamwhistle also does an excellent job of tying their product to the location in which it is brewed. It is paramount that our beer embodies something of the region, that the consumer feels a tangible connection between beverage and place."

To start, Western Newfoundland Brewing devoted itself to producing and mastering two brews: Wild Cove Cream Ale and Killdevil Pale Ale. As a nanobrewery, you won't find their beers in stores any time soon, but it is a long term goal to be available in NLC outlets throughout the island.

For now, try them on the West Coast at Galliott Studios in Woody Point, The Anchor Pub in Rocky Harbour, The Cat Stop in Norris Point, Madison's Restaurant in Steady Brook, or Sorrento Restaurant and Marble Mountain in Corner Brook, as well as Jack Axes in St. John's.

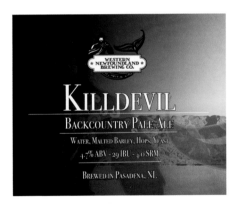

Killdevil Pale Ale

ABV & TYPE: 4.5% Pale Ale

APPEARANCE: Light and sunshine-bright in colour with a robust and luscious creamy head to "protect the golden draught beneath"

AROMA: There's a delicate fragrance of stone-fruit off the top, and a scent of fresh-baked bread to foreshadow the deeper malt flavours

TEXTURE: Full in body and "pleasant to hold in the mouth as you explore the taste and texture for some time before depositing to the gullet"

TASTE: Generously hopped for tangy flavours of grapefruit and apricot at the start, and pine carrying the end. Moderately bitter. "As Killdevil traverses the palate," says the brewery's Jim MacDonald, "the faintest notes of fresh, white bread are released from our enthusiastic use of Vienna malt"

BEHIND THE BEER: Killdevil Pale Ale is named after Killdevil Mountain, along the beautiful shore of Bonne Bay on the Viking Trail. "It's a beautiful old mountain that has a habit of catching the evening light in the most spectacular manner," Jim says, "much like how this brew captures sunlight in a spectacular manner."

Pale ales are a beloved style among beer lovers, but they didn't want to make a run-of-the-mill pale ale. Western Newfoundland Brewing wanted to make sure theirs stood out and above the crowd. They wanted a lot going on, they wanted all aspects of the experience, "from nose to aftertaste" to be thoroughly enjoyable. "We want people to look forward to that next sip."

In Killdevil Pale Ale, "only two varieties of lightly kilned premium malts are used." As far as the hops go, "Centennial, Citra, and Mosaic hops are used for moderate bittering, but employed generously at the flavour and dry-hopped stages."

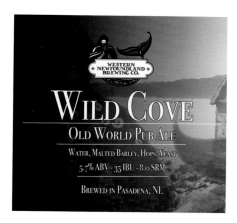

WESTERN NEWFOUNDLAND BREWING CO.

WILD COVE
OLD WORLD PUB ALE

WATER, MALTED BARLEY, HOPS, YEAST

5.7% ABV - 35 IBU - 8.0 SRM

BREWED IN PASADENA, NL

Wild Cove Cream Ale

ABV & TYPE: 5.3% Cream Ale

APPEARANCE: Tawny copper in colour, with a dense and creamy head of a nice complementary colour sheltering the liquid below

AROMA: "The spiciness of Tettnang blends elegantly with the baker's scents of our beloved Munich"

TEXTURE: Smooth and full-bodied

TASTE: Bready with herbal, spicy notes from the Pale and Munich malts and moderately applied Nugget and Tettnang hops. "Our unorthodox mashing process extracts a wide-range of full-flavoured proteins, sugars, and vitamins." This beer is malt-forward, though still dry

BEHIND THE BEER: The story behind this beer's origin is quite literally unbelievable. According to its brewers, it's "a little known fact" that the recipe was handed down to them by Murphy the Mersasquatch. If you've not heard of the elusive

Mersasquatch, it's a "half-merperson (bottom) and half-sasquatch (top)," and found exclusively in northern Gros Morne.

"Murphy lives in a cabin found deep in the backcountry of the Long Range Mountains," they told us, "and is almost never observed by human eyes." Their brewmaster "was lucky enough to meet him one day while on a hike near Western Brook Pond."

The two got to chatting when Norm turned to Murphy, "There are two strawberries. One turns to the other and says, 'You know, if you hadn't been so fresh last night, we wouldn't be in this jam.'" Murphy reportedly howled as only a Mersasquatch can, and as a show of gratitude for the knee-slapper of a joke, Murphy gifted Norm his age-old beer recipes, "So long as Norm helped carry the legend of the Mersasquatch to all corners of Newfoundland and Labrador."

Murphy then, "as gracefully as a fish-monkey can, flopped himself back into the deep woods, never to be seen again. For this reason we have adopted Murphy the Mersasquatch as our mascot, and his image is now featured front and centre in our logo and all branded artwork."

Anyway, the beer. It's a smooth yet full bodied cream ale. "Were it appropriate to say so," says the brewery's Jim MacDonald, "this may be a suitable breakfast replacement."

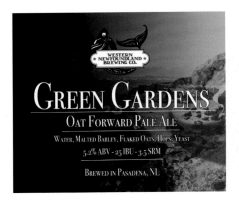

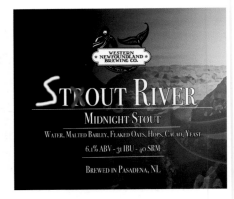

Green Gardens Haze

ABV & TYPE: 5.2% Pale Ale

APPEARANCE: Having not tried this one before publishing this book, we'll take the brewery's word for it: "Golden honeybees mating on a daisy."

AROMA: "Peaches and Cream at dawn," they call it

TEXTURE: Full bodied, "and a wee bit viscous"

TASTE: Citrus and honey off the top, and fresh-baked oat bread to finish

BEHIND THE BEER: Named after one of Gros Morne National Park's famed hiking trails, the brewery developed this beer specifically "to be enjoyed on a sunny but not-too-hot Western Newfoundland day. Beer lovers love it. Non-beer lovers love it. Everyone loves it."

Stout River

ABV & TYPE: 6.1% Stout

APPEARANCE: Straight from the horse's mouth, "A chroma desaturation vortex"

AROMA: Dark dark chocolate, and dark dark coffee

TEXTURE: Smooth and light on the palate

TASTE: They say it's "80% cacao fine dark chocolate, paired with an espresso"

BEHIND THE BEER: See what they did there? Instead of Trout River, it is Stout River. The brewery wanted a stout with no astringent after taste, "thick as we can muster, but still light on the belly." Sounds like a magic stout recipe. They say the dry coffee and cacao notes make the drinker wonder if this is a beer at all, hence their dubbing it "a superhero's breakfast."

Index

Photo Credits

BREAKWATER
P.O. Box 2188, St. John's, NL, Canada, A1C 6E6
WWW.BREAKWATERBOOKS.COM

A CIP catalogue record for this book is available from Library and Archives Canada.
Copyright © 2018 The Overcast
ISBN 978-1-55081-659-4

We acknowledge the support of the Canada Council for the Arts, which last year
invested $153 million to bring the arts to Canadians throughout the country.
We acknowledge the financial support of the Government of Canada and the
Government of Newfoundland and Labrador through the Department of Tourism,
Culture, Industry and Innovation for our publishing activities.
PRINTED AND BOUND IN CANADA.

 Canada Council
for the Arts   Conseil des Arts
du Canada   Canadä   Newfoundland
Labrador

Breakwater Books is committed to choosing papers and materials for our books
that help to protect our environment. To this end, this book is printed on a recycled
paper that is certified by the Forest Stewardship Council®.